Sunday School Lessons

from the

Apostle Paul's

Letter to the

ROMANS

COMMENTARIES AND LESSONS BY

LARRY D. ALEXANDER

Second Edition

A WIFE'S REFLECTIONS

I remember when Larry first started teaching Sunday school and how the HOLY SPIRIT took hold of him, through his studies. I watched the HOLY SPIRIT change him, as even our marital relationship got better. After he received his calling to teach, he spent an enormous amount of time (and still does) preparing for his class. The more the class grew, the more time he seemed to spend with the LORD in his studies.

I believe his students inspire him more than any other earthly factor, and I believe that is what inspired him to begin writing Sunday school lesson commentaries and ultimately, writing these books. The books that he has written are very practical and should be shared around the world.

The lessons teach that we are responsible to have a personal relationship with the LORD, and the personal applications always cause us to reflect on ourselves as being responsible Christians. He wants us to look in the mirror so that we can identify the source of our problems, and then, look to GOD so that HE can help us to solve them.

Patricia Alexander

CONTENTS

CONTENTS

I

INTRODUCTION

Larry D. Alexander is a well-known visual artist, turned Christian teacher and author, who was called by GOD, more than 15 years ago, to learn and teach HIS Holy Word, without help from the institutions of men. He understood his calling to be that his training in the Word was to be infused in him, through direct guidance from GOD, through the HOLY SPIRIT, and that GOD will always lead him spiritually to the right material, people, and sources that he needs, in order to successfully do HIS Will. Alexander says GOD instructed him to began to write down, and retain in writing, those things that he had learned, and then, to share them with others. Alexander has been teaching Sunday school and bible studies for the past 14 years.

This book is written to help revive the interest of adults in building themselves up in the Word of GOD by attending Home and Church Bible studies and Sunday school classes in their respective Christian churches, and, to start up, or restore Bible studies and Sunday school classes back to those Christian churches that are lacking these opportunities to get to know CHRIST JESUS, our LORD. Alexander strongly believes that the only thing that can change a man or woman for the better is the Word of GOD.

This is the third book written and published by Alexander since 2006. It consists of 21 Sunday school lessons from the book of Romans, and should not be confused with his book *Home and Church Bible Study Commentaries from Paul's letter to the Romans* which is a complete commentary from the book of Romans, and a part of his Home And Church Bible Study Series. All of his books are designed to promote spiritual growth and right-living in those who choose to read and incorporate GOD's directives into their everyday lives.

The teaching commentaries that are presented in this book, as well as Alexander's previous books are bold and straightforward. They are to be used to help introduce people to JESUS through a study of the words and actions that were demonstrated to us by JESUS, during HIS three-year ministry here on earth, and, through the work of the Apostle Paul and others, who were instrumental in the development and establishment of the early Christian Church. There is a strong focus on developing good Christian living practices and behavior, and, on developing a fear and reverence for the ONLY WISE GOD, WHO is our SAVIOR, through JESUS CHRIST, HIS SON, WHO sent to us, the HOLY SPIRIT.

II

INTRODUCTION TO THE BOOK OF ROMANS

Paul's letter to the Romans is the most formal and systematic of his New Testament epistles. In fact, it has been called, and, is considered to be, the theological cornerstone of the New Testament. The main theme of this letter is that "righteousness" is a free gift from GOD, and is only receivable by "faith". Paul wrote this letter to introduce himself to the Church at Rome, and to give them a summary of Christian teaching.

He begins by showing them how every person has rebelled against GOD, and is cut off from HIM because of sin. Paul also demonstrates in this letter how GOD, through HIS mercy, interceded, while we were yet set against HIM in full-fledged sin. GOD, then, opened the way back up to HIMSELF through CHRIST JESUS, and now, anyone who trusts in JESUS will be saved from evil, and be given the power of GOD, through the HOLY SPIRIT, to live a good life.

Paul goes on to explain what a new life in CHRIST should consist of, and, how a person no longer needs to live under the dominion of sin and death. Anyone, who becomes a believer is liberated by the SPIRIT of GOD, and thereby, has eternal peace from within.

First and foremost, I suppose this letter by Paul is an explanation of how GOD justifies us as sinners, when we choose to live in CHRIST. In fact, HE not only justifies us, but HE actually makes us just (Romans 5:19). HE then treats us as if we had never sinned at all, and HE expects us to enter into a life-long period of sanctification, whereby we will sin less and less, as we move along in our Christian walk.

Only GOD can transform the sinful person and make him, or her, into someone who can reflect HIS image to others through their behavior. Paul's letter to the Romans answers the most difficult questions about the first advent of CHRIST, HIS crucifixion, and, HIS resurrection. Most scholars believe this letter was written circa A.D. 58, while he was still in Corinth, and several years before his first imprisonment in Rome.

This letter served to resolve most of the tensions in the Roman Church at that time, as it answered questions regarding the harmony of GOD's word as a whole. Paul insists that, being righteous requires us to actually be more like CHRIST, and not just conform to oral or written law. We must be more like HIM in our motives, and, in our deeds. Paul had a great dream in his heart, as well as, a great plan on his mind for spreading Christianity. And he felt that he needed to win Rome over as an important base of operation, if, he was to be successful in the western world.

LESSON ONE:

REVEALING GOD'S RIGHTEOUSNESS
(GOD's power to save lives comes through the gospels)

SCRIPTURE:
The King James Version
(Romans 1:1-17)

1 **(1)** Paul, a servant of JESUS CHRIST, called to be an apostle, separated unto the gospel of GOD. **(2)** (Which HE had promised afore by HIS prophets in the Holy Scriptures,) **(3)** Concerning HIS SON JESUS CHRIST our LORD, which was made of the seed of David according to the flesh; **(4)** And declared to be the SON of GOD with power, according to the SPIRIT OF HOLINESS, by the resurrection from the dead: **(5)** By WHOM we have received grace and apostleship, for obedience to the faith among all nations, for HIS name: **(6)** Among WHOM are ye also the called of JESUS CHRIST: **(7)** To all that be in Rome, beloved of GOD, called to be saints: Grace to you and peace from GOD our FATHER, and the LORD JESUS CHRIST. **(8)** First, I thank my GOD through JESUS CHRIST for you all, that your faith is spoken of throughout the whole world. **(9)** For GOD is my witness, WHOM I serve with my spirit in the gospel of HIS SON, that without ceasing I make mention of you always in my prayers; **(10)** Making request, if by any means now at length I might have a prosperous journey by the will of GOD to come unto you. **(11)** For I long to see you, that I may impart unto you some spiritual gift, to the end ye may be established; **(12)** That is, that I may be comforted together with you by the mutual faith both of you and me. **(13)** Now I would not have you ignorant, brethren, that oftentimes I purposed to come unto you, (but was let hitherto,) that I might have some fruit among you also, even as among other Gentiles. **(14)** I am debtor both to the Greeks, and to the Barbarians; both to the wise, and to the unwise. **(15)** So, as much as in me is, I am ready to preach the gospel to you that are at Rome also. **(16)** For I am not ashamed of the gospel of CHRIST: for it is the power of GOD unto salvation to every one that believeth; to the Jew first, and also to the Greek. **(17)** For therein is the righteousness of GOD revealed from faith to faith: as it is written, "The just shall live by faith".

COMMENTARY:

When Paul wrote his, now famous, letter to the Romans, he had not yet visited the church in Rome. He wrote Romans shortly before his visit to Jerusalem, where he went to deliver a monetary gift from the Gentiles (Acts 24:17 & Rom. 15:25). At that time, he was residing in Corinth as a guest in the home of Gaius, while visiting the church at Cenchrea. He resided there for three months according to Acts 20:2-3, and so this letter was most likely written there, probably during the early spring of A.D. 58.

In the biblical Greek, the word used for "Apostle" is "Apostolos" (Ap-os-tol-os), and it is "an ambassador, or commissioner of CHRIST", or, "he that is sent". In the New Testament, the title "Apostle" refers to the leaders of the early church, who, had witnessed the risen CHRIST, and were specially commissioned by HIM personally to preach the Gospel (Acts 1:21-22). JESUS originally gave the title to the twelve original disciples (Luke 6:13), however, after HIS resurrection, the term was applied to a wider circle of preachers and witnesses who also seen HIM after HIS resurrection (Acts 14:4 & 14).

Paul's claim to be an Apostle was challenged by some at first, mostly because of his previous history of persecuting Christians in and around Rome. However, Paul staked his Apostleship claim on the basis of his direct call by JESUS when HE appeared to him, while traveling on the road to Damascus (Acts 9:1-9). In his letters, Paul refers to himself as being a "slave" of JESUS CHRIST, or, in the original Greek, a "doulos" (doo-los). "Doulos", or "Slave", is the proudest title of the ancient Prophets. It is a title that, they felt, separated them from all other men, the fact that they were "slaves of GOD".

We must be careful to remember however, that, for every man, (not just the apostles) GOD has a purpose, and no man's life is without that purpose. In fact, it is for the purpose of GOD that all Christians are called, and all creation is made. It is also by the work of HIS HOLY SPIRIT that a life is hallowed towards HIM, and, it is because of the spilling of the blood of HIS SON, CHRIST JESUS, that our past sins are forgiven us, and we, like Paul, can look forward to a future of obedience to GOD.

Through the Gospel, JESUS saved Paul that day on the road to Damascus, and Paul's life was forever changed for the better because of it. But isn't that what JESUS does for each of us, through HIS vicarious sacrifice? HE saves us, from permanent separation from GOD.

Paul was always ready to preach the Gospel to whoever would listen, because he knew about the saving power of the word of GOD. He placed no faith in his own abilities, because he understood that the life-changing power was contained in the Scriptures. In fact, GOD's very being is wrapped up in HIS Word, and, because of it, HIS Word manifests to us, GOD HIMSELF. Scripture is not just a composition of GOD's instructions, or how HE deals with man, but rather, it is the power that can redeem us from the hopelessness of our own self-imposed circumstances.

Let us remember that, by the time Paul is writing this letter to the Romans, he has already been imprisoned in Philippi, chased out of Thessalonica, smuggled out of Berea, laughed at in Athens, and in Corinth, his message was considered to be ludicrous to the Greeks, and a stumbling block to the Jews. Yet in Romans 1:16-17, he declares in one of his most famous statements that, "I am not ashamed of the Gospel of CHRIST: for it is the power of GOD unto salvation to everyone that believeth; to the Jew first, and also to the Greek. For therein is the righteousness of GOD revealed, from faith to faith: as it is written, the just shall live by faith".

GOD intended for HIS Gospel to be for all people, Jews and Gentiles, in fact, the Church in Rome, at that time, was made up mostly of Gentile Christians who had answered the call of the Gospel of CHRIST. Through the work of the HOLY SPIRIT, all believers become Saints, and are therefore GOD's holy people. Paul was not ashamed of the Gospel, and neither should we be. For, it unleashes the power of GOD that brings all mankind to salvation, and, in simpler terms, it saves us from ourselves.

PERSONAL APPLICATION:

(1). If you have not accepted the wonderful gift of Salvation, talk to someone, whom you know to be a Christian, about how you should go about it.

(2). If you have already accepted CHRIST, sit down right now and write a thank-you note to GOD for giving you the most precious part of HIMSELF, CHRIST JESUS.

(3). As long as there is breath in your body, it is not too late to accept Salvation. The right time to come to CHRIST, is always right now, and the right way to come to CHRIST is always, just as you are.

LIFE RESPONSE:

Pray a prayer of thanks to GOD each day for Salvation, through CHRIST JESUS. Pray also that people everywhere will clearly hear and understand the gospel message and be able to share in the gift of Eternal Life.

KEY VERSE: Romans 1:16

DEVOTIONAL PASSAGES: John 6:35, John 8:12, John 10:11

LESSON TWO:

GOD'S ANGER AT SIN
(GOD shows HIS anger from Heaven against the sinful and the wicked)

SCRIPTURE:
The King James Version
(Romans 1:18-32)

1 **(18)** For the wrath of GOD is revealed from Heaven against all ungodliness and unrighteousness of men, who hold the truth in unrighteousness; **(19)** Because that which may be known of GOD is manifest in them; for GOD hath shewed it unto them. **(20)** For the invisible things of HIM from the creation of the world are clearly seen, being understood by the things that are made, even HIS eternal power and GODHEAD; so that they are without excuse: **(21)** Because that, when they knew GOD, they glorified HIM not as GOD, neither were thankful; but became vain in their imaginations, and their foolish heart was darkened. **(22)** Professing themselves to be wise, they became fools, **(23)** And changed the glory of the uncorruptible GOD into an image made like to corruptible man, and to birds, and fourfooted beasts, and creeping things. **(24)** Wherefore GOD also gave them up to uncleanness through the lusts of their own hearts, to dishonour their own bodies between themselves: **(25)** Who changed the truth of GOD into a lie, and worshipped and served the creature more than the creator, who is blessed for ever. Amen. **(26)** For this cause GOD gave them up unto vile affections: for even their women did change the natural use into that which is against nature: **(27)** And likewise also the men, leaving the natural use of the woman, burned in their lust one toward another; men with men working that which is unseemly, and receiving in themselves that recompence of their error which was meet. **(28)** And even as they did not like to retain GOD in their knowledge, GOD gave them over to a reprobate mind, to do those things which are not convenient; **(29)** Being filled with all unrighteousness, fornication, wickedness, covetousness, maliciousness; full of envy, murder, debate, deceit, malignity; whisperers, **(30)** Backbiters, haters of GOD, despiteful, proud, boasters, inventors of evil things, disobedient to parents, **(31)** Without understanding, covenantbreakers, without natural affection, implacable, unmerciful: **(32)** Who knowing the judgment of GOD, that they which commit such things are worthy of death, not only do the same, but have pleasure in them that do them.

COMMENTARY:

Failure to give reverence to GOD will ultimately result in our failure to treat each other right as human beings made in the image of GOD. The reason why the gospel must be preached is because we, as human beings, continue to suppress the truth about GOD, and, the truth about ourselves. In Romans 1:18-32, Paul shifts gears, from talking about the kind of relationship into which a person can enter into with GOD by faith, to the kind of wrath we can expect to incur if we are intentionally blind to GOD the CREATOR, and choose to worship our own ideas, and, those things which are created by GOD, instead of GOD the creator, HIMSELF.

To the biblical prophets, the wrath of GOD was a perpetual event that would only culminate, or peak, in terror and destruction in "The Last Day", or coming "Day of the LORD". Remember, in biblical times, whenever Israel strayed away from GOD too long, HIS wrath would come against them and whip them back into line with HIS thinking.

And so, we must understand that GOD's wrath will always, even today, visit us before too long. Our human sinfulness is seen quite vividly through our wicked acts, but it is also seen in the way we view and respond to GOD day by day. When we publicly and privately approve things that we know are contrary to GOD's laws, we show HIM disrespect and rejection. We reject GOD morally through homosexual and adulterous behavior. We reject HIM in our character through greed and wickedness. And we also reject HIM in our relationships by way of envy, murder, deceit, and malice.

GOD's generous offer of salvation is sorely needed by each of us, and, we do, after all, stand rightly deserving of HIS divine wrath and judgment instead. Most of mankind has rejected GOD, because they simply reject the knowledge of HIM that is available to us through HIS Holy and divine Scriptures. It is very much incumbent upon each of us to pick up GOD's Word daily, read it, and study it, so that we can come to understand plainly, GOD's Will, and how that Will should play a role in our personal lives.

We can all see, quite clearly, GOD's invisible qualities of divine nature and eternal power, both through HIS creation, and through HIS Holy Word, and GOD shared HIS "invisible qualities", or, "divine nature" with us, when HE first created mankind, all those years ago (Rom. 1:20). Those invisible qualities, or, "Communicable Attributes", that make up GOD's divine nature are, Life, Personality, Truth, Wisdom, Love, Justice, and Holiness. Those attributes are what make it possible for man, out of all of GOD's creation, to have a personal, experiential relationship with HIM, and thereby, we have no excuse for not knowing GOD (Rom. 1:20), or obeying GOD, even before we received the HOLY SPIRIT as Christians (see Rom. 2:14).

Remember, the HOLY SPIRIT, scripture tells us (Matt. 3:16, Mark 1:10, Luke 3:21-22, & John 1:32-34), did not come upon JESUS until HE was around thirty years old, and HE had perfectly obeyed GOD up to that point, as a 100 percent human being, the same way that we are born. JESUS came to show us first, how it is possible to obey GOD in our natural born state, if we choose to. GOD did not trick us by sending us a "supernatural being" to show us how to live as a "human being", under HIM, here on earth. HE actually sent JESUS here to function first as a 100% human being in order to show us that we, as 100% humans, can choose to live a life of total obedience to GOD, simply because HE had already placed HIS divine nature in us from the beginning of time.

GOD is angry at our sin because HE knows that HE made us to do better, for HE made us in HIS OWN "spiritual" image. GOD wouldn't have been angry at the people of the Old Testament for their sins, if they couldn't do any better, or, couldn't help but sin. GOD, from the beginning, made us to be like HIM, spiritually. We know this because JESUS says, "GOD is SPIRIT" (John 4:24) and therefore, this means that GOD doesn't have a physical image. In Genesis 1:26, where GOD says "Let us make man in our Image" HE was not speaking of a "physical image", but rather, a "spiritual image" consisting of those seven "Communicable Attributes" that I mentioned earlier. They are the "invisible qualities" that Paul speaks of here in Romans 1:20 that, make us look like the GOD WHO created us, spiritually. HE supplied us with those attributes so that we would be able to worship HIM, have a personal, experiential, compatible relationship with HIM, and, in fact, could be like HIM.

We've all lived a sinful life since Adam, but it was because we chose to, not because we couldn't help it, as most of us want to believe. And we want to believe that because, in our sinful minds, it gives us a palatable excuse to continue to do wrong. However, if we continue to persist in doing wrong things, then, GOD will eventually turn us over to our own shameful desires. And, at that time, our lives will become filled with all manner of wickedness, and we will even begin to invent new ways to sin, in order to enhance our pleasure (Vs 24-31).

And, even though we are aware of GOD's death penalty (permanent separation from HIM), because we have, by then, developed a reprobated mind, we will continue on in our sin, and even begin to encourage others to sin also (v. 32). The sin, and sometimes, amoral attitudes, that permeates our society today, and makes our lives so painful to endure, is nothing more than divine judgment on us for rejecting GOD, and choosing immorality over GOD. Our iniquities vividly express our sinful nature, a nature that is adverse to the nature that GOD originally gave us. And it automatically, brings about GOD's wrath, and subsequent, divine judgment, not just on "The Last Day", but also, in this day that we currently live in.

PERSONAL APPLICATION:

(1). Look in the mirror and ask yourself, "Are you better off following your own plan, of taking matters into your own hands, or, are you ready to try something that really will work in making your life more worth living?
(2). Try GOD, our SAVIOR, through JESUS CHRIST.
(3). You've already seen what life is like without GOD, now all you need to do is accept CHRIST JESUS and all that comes with HIM, to make your life a complete success, both now, and forever.

LIFE RESPONSE:

Pray this prayer: LORD JESUS I need YOU. I thank YOU for dying on the cross for my sins. I do earnestly repent for my trespasses against YOU. And I open up the door to my heart, and invite YOU in, as my LORD and SAVIOR. I thank YOU for forgiving my sins, and then offering me Eternal Life. I accept YOUR offer of Salvation, and I want YOU to take control of the throne of my life, and, make me into the kind of person that YOU want me to be. Thank YOU JESUS. Amen.

KEY VERSE: Romans 1:18

DEVOTIONAL PASSAGES: Matthew 11:28-30, John 11:25-26, John 14:1-3

PRIVILEGE AND RESPONSIBILITY
(True Jews, Christians, and the law)

SCRIPTURE:
The King James Version
(Romans 2:17-29)

2 **(17)** Behold, thou art called a Jew, and restest in the law, and makest thy boast of GOD, **(18)** And knowest HIS will, and approvest the things that are more excellent, being instructed out of the law; **(19)** And art confident that thou thyself art a guide of the blind, a light of them which are in darkness, **(20)** An instructor of the foolish, a teacher of babes, which hast the form of knowledge and of the truth in the law. **(21)** Thou therefore which teachest another, teachest thou not thyself? Thou that preachest a man should not steal, dost thou steal? **(22)** Thou that sayest a man should not commit adultery, dost thou commit adultery? Thou that abhorrest idols, dost thou commit sacrilege? **(23)** Thou that makest thy boast of the law, through breaking the law dishonourest thou GOD? **(24)** For the name of GOD is blasphemed among the Gentiles through you, as it is written. **(25)** For circumcision verily profiteth, if thou keep the law: but if thou be a breaker of the law, thy circumcision is made uncircumcision. **(26)** Therefore if the uncircumcision keep the righteousness of the law, shall not his uncircumcision be counted for circumcision? **(27)** And shall not uncircumcision which is by nature, if it fulfill the law, judge thee, who by the letter and circumcision dost transgress the law? **(28)** For he is not a Jew, which is one outwardly; neither is that circumcision, which is outward in the flesh: **(29)** But he is a Jew, which is one inwardly; and circumcision is that of the heart, in the SPIRIT, and not in the letter; whose praise is not of men, but of GOD.

COMMENTARY:

In Romans 2:17-29, Paul takes a look at the basis for which Jews claimed spiritual superiority over Gentiles in those days. He shows how both, as human beings, break the law of GOD, and how the claim of superiority by the Jews amounts only to an expression of raw pride and unwitting ignorance on their part.

To the Jews, an announcement such as this must have been quite hard to hear and take in those days. They were absolutely certain that GOD regarded them with special favor simply because of their national origin, or descent from Abraham. Remember Abraham is the towering figure, to which the Jews traced their origins, as GOD's chosen people. They saw it as a "privilege" to be born Jewish, but never did quite grasp the "responsibility", in being the "light to the world", that their Jewish birthright carried with it.

Here Paul shows how a relationship with GOD requires an inner spiritual circumcision of the heart, not just the outward, physical act of the circumcision of the male's genital to be a member of GOD's covenant community. Paul reminded them that circumcision only meant something, if they obeyed GOD's law, and, if they didn't obey GOD's law, they were no better off spiritually than the uncircumcised Gentiles. Paul insists that they were not true Jews, unless their hearts were right with GOD (v.29). In fact, an uncircumcised Gentile, who kept GOD's law, was much better off than a circumcised Jew who didn't (v.27).

In the Greek, the word Paul uses for "praise" in verse 29 is "epainos" (ep-ahee-nos), and it is "a laudable or commendable thing". Here Paul is saying that only GOD determines the righteousness of men, not other men. GOD's promises are not to people of a certain race, or to people who bear a certain mark on their bodies. HIS promises are to those who believe HIM, and exemplify it through their lifestyles and behavior. Therefore, it is not a matter of pedigree, but rather, it is a matter of character. We must be right with GOD in our living, regardless, of our race. In other words, Jews and Gentiles, in order to please GOD, must act like Christians, in both their private, and public life, at all times.

PERSONAL APPLICATION:

(1). Remember, the real mark of your relationship with GOD is on the inside. It is a circumcision of the heart that is performed by the HOLY SPIRIT, that sets a person apart from the world.
(2). Your moral nature is the only thing that will ever testify about you to GOD, and your acts are the only real measure of your morality.
(3). When our personal history judges us, it will be looking to see if we were, in our lifetimes, rightly related to CHRIST, rightly related to each other as Christians, and, rightly related to the world.

LIFE RESPONSE:

Pray daily that you will, at all times, show proper reverence for CHRIST, proper love for your fellowman, and maintain the desire and strength, through CHRIST, to not lose your heart to people and things of this world.

KEY VERSE: Roman 2:29

DEVOTIONAL PASSAGES: John 15:1-16:4, Matthew 25:31-46, Acts 10:34-48

GIFT OF GRACE AND JUSTIFICATION
(All sin offends GOD)

SCRIPTURE:
The King James Version
(Romans 3:1-4 & 19-31)

3 **(1)** What advantage then hath the Jew? or what profit is there of circumcision? **(2)** Much every way: chiefly, because that unto them were committed the oracles of GOD. **(3)** For what if some did not believe? shall their unbelief make the faith of GOD without effect? **(4)** GOD forbid: yea, let GOD be true, but every man a liar; as it is written, that thou mightest be justified in thy sayings, and mightest overcome when thou art judged. **(19)** Now we know that what things so ever the law saith, it saith to them who are under the law: that every mouth may be stopped, and all the world may become guilty before GOD. **(20)** Therefore by the deeds of the law there shall no flesh be justified in HIS sight: for by the law is the knowledge of sin. **(21)** But now the righteousness of GOD without the law is manifested, being witnessed by the law and the prophets; **(22)** Even the righteousness of GOD which is by faith of JESUS CHRIST unto all and upon all them that believe: for there is no difference: **(23)** For all have sinned, and come short of the glory of GOD. **(24)** Being justified freely by HIS grace through the redemption that is in CHRIST JESUS: **(25)** Whom GOD hath set forth to be a propitiation through faith in HIS blood, to declare HIS righteousness for the remission of sins that are past, through the forbearance of GOD. **(26)** To declare, I say, at this time HIS righteousness: that HE might be just, and the JUSTIFIER of him which believeth in JESUS. **(27)** Where is boasting then? It is excluded. By what law? Of works? Nay: but by the law of faith. **(28)** Therefore we conclude that a man is justified by faith without the deeds of the law. **(29)** Is HE the GOD of the Jews only? is HE not also of the Gentiles? Yes, of the Gentiles also: **(30)** Seeing it is one GOD, which shall justify the circumcision by faith, and uncircumcision through faith. **(31)** Do we then make void the law through faith? GOD forbid: yea, we establish the law.

COMMENTARY:

In the Greek, the word Paul uses for "justification" is "dikaiosune" (dik-ah-yos-oo-nay), and it is "equity in character or action", or, "righteousness". In the biblical sense, the word "Justification" has a dual meaning. It means that a person is pronounced "not guilty" before GOD, and, that the same person is pronounced "righteous".

Justification is a one-time event that happens at the very moment of one receiving "Salvation" from GOD. Then, the process of "Sanctification" begins. Sanctification is a lifelong process, by which the "saved" person is expected to become more like CHRIST, with each passing day, in terms to their behavior.

The great advantage the Jews had, at one time, was that they had possession of GOD's word, and more often than not, they chose not to obey it. Thanks to GOD's grace, a lack of faith by them, did not nullify HIS faithfulness. GOD's law is not intended to save us, but rather, it is intended to make us aware of our sins. GOD, through the Scriptures, has revealed a righteousness that has nothing to do with the law. And since all have sinned, and fallen short of the glory of GOD, all need to be justified by a "Grace Gift" given only to those who have faith in JESUS CHRIST.

The Jews often misunderstood the meaning of their special position with GOD. Paul believed it was special because with it came a certain responsibility. He knew the special position didn't afford them to do what "they" like, but rather, it afforded them with a responsibility to do what GOD likes. In verse 2 of this passage, the word Paul uses for the phrase "oracles of GOD", in his original writings, is "logia", and it is "a special statement, or pronouncement from GOD". Here it means the "Ten Commandments", and here in verses 2-3, Paul is saying that GOD entrusted the Jews with keeping the Ten Commandments, not with special privileges.

The Jews never quite grasped the fact that, GOD's "special choice" of them, was made for the purpose of "special duty" and responsibility to HIM. Responsibility is always the "obverse" of privilege. The more opportunity a person has to do right, the greater their condemnation is, when they chose to do wrong. The root of all sin is disobedience. When pride sets the "will of man" against the "Will of GOD", the end result is always "sin".

When a person has sinned, they sometimes display an amazing ingenuity to justify it. In verse 26 of this third chapter of Romans, we see a good and gracious paradox. Paul tells us that GOD is just and fair, and that, in that incredible, miraculous grace that JESUS came to bring us, GOD accepts the sinner, not as a criminal, but as a son whom HE still loves.

Remember, obedience to the laws of GOD is what we can do for ourselves. Grace is concerned with what GOD can do, and, is doing for us. The laws of GOD serve to show us, just how far we are from HIS high and glorious standards. It exposes things to us that we didn't even know were sins. The law shows us, very vividly, our need for grace, and, a SAVIOR. GOD's grace gives us a chance to escape the bondage of sin. There is nothing good in our own flesh. The only way for us to be reconciled to GOD is through grace received as a result of our belief in our LORD and SAVIOR, JESUS CHRIST.

PERSONAL APPLICATION:

(1). Remember, all of our human acts are tainted by our own sin nature, and thereby, less than prefect, and not acceptable to GOD.

(2). GOD's Law serves to show us our imperfections, and when we are measured by HIS glorious standard, we all come up short.

(3). Everyone has already been judged by GOD's Law and the verdict has been announced by GOD as guilty.

(4). Our righteousness, or justification can never come from our own acts, it can only come from the acts of GOD.

LIFE RESPONSE:

Pray daily and thank GOD for HIS propitiating sacrifice to us, through our LORD and SAVIOR, JESUS CHRIST. Amen.

KEY VERSES: Romans 3:23-24

DEVOTIONAL PASSAGES: Ephesians 1:3-14, Ephesians 2:1-10, Romans 3:21-31

LESSON FIVE:

(15)

INHERITORS OF GOD'S PROMISES
(Faith is believing, that GOD will keep HIS promises)

SCRIPTURE:
The King James Version
(Romans 4:2-3 & 13-25)

4 **(2)** For if Abraham were justified by works, he hath whereof to glory; but not before GOD. **(3)** For what saith the Scripture? Abraham believed GOD, and it was counted unto him for righteousness. **(13)** For the promise, that he should be the heir of the world, was not to Abraham, or to his seed, through the Law, but through the righteousness of faith. **(14)** For if they which are of the Law be heirs, faith is made void, and the promise made of none effect: **(15)** Because the Law worketh wrath: for where no Law is, there is no transgression. **(16)** Therefore it is of faith, that it might be by Grace; to the end the promise might be sure to all the seed; not to that only which is of the Law, but to that also which is of the faith of Abraham; who is the father of us all, **(17)** (As it is written, "I have made thee a father of many nations",) before HIM WHOM he believed, even GOD, WHO quickeneth the dead, and calleth those things which be not as though they were. **(18)** Who against hope believed in hope, that he might become the father of many nations, according to that which was spoken, "So shall thy seed be". **(19)** And being not weak in faith, he considered not his own body now dead, when he was about an hundred years old, neither yet the deadness of Sarah's womb: **(20)** He staggered not at the promise of GOD through unbelief; but was strong in faith, giving glory to GOD; **(21)** And being fully persuaded that, what HE had promised, HE was able also to perform. **(22)** And therefore it was imputed to him for righteousness. **(23)** Now it was not written for his sake alone, that it was imputed to him; **(24)** But for us also, to whom it shall be imputed, if we believe on HIM that raised up JESUS our LORD from the dead; **(25)** Who was delivered for our offences, and was raised again for our justification.

COMMENTARY:

In the first century, many Jews believed that Paul's teachings on grace and salvation by faith, seriously undermined the Mosaic Law, and thus, denied GOD's

Old Testament revelation to man. Paul argued instead, that, the Gospel he taught only served to uphold the Law, and to give it the place that GOD always intended for it to have.

In Romans chapter 3, taking up at verse 28, Paul sets out to educate the early Christian Church in Rome and other places on how GOD's grace and salvation through JESUS CHRIST actually establishes the Law in GOD's intended role, which is to be a mirror that can, first, show us our sins, and then, point us toward faith.

In the Greek, the word New Testament writers use for "faith" is "pistis", and it means "to rely upon with an inward certainty". Even before the Law, there was Faith. And as I mentioned in my commentaries on the previous chapter, Abraham is the towering figure to whom the Jews traced their origins and special place as GOD's chosen people. By quoting Genesis 15:6, here in verse 3 of chapter 4, Paul is able to prove to the Jews that the roots of faith are anchored in an "imputed", rather than "earned" righteousness.

Here Paul demonstrates from sacred history, that, salvation always has been a gift of GOD received through faith, and that, faith is the way by which Abraham received his salvation, even before there was a Law, or a "Ten Commandments". Righteousness was accredited to Abraham, because he had faith, and he believed GOD (4:1-3).

In the biblical Greek, there is a wonderful sounding word that New Testament writers use for "promise". It is "epaggelia" (ep-ang-el-ee-ah), and it is "an announcement of divine assurance of good". In Romans 4:13-17, Paul argues that, the "promise" of GOD was given to Abraham because of his "faith". And since the promises that are given to him, and, to his offspring are rooted in faith, and not, in the law, the Jews then, must also rely on faith, rather than works, in order to please GOD, and continue to receive HIS "promised goodness".

Abraham was confident that GOD was able to do that which HE had promised, and, that HE would surely keep HIS word. Whenever we believe GOD's promise of salvation through JESUS CHRIST, we too, are accredited with "righteousness" that we did not, or could not earn on our own (Romans 4:18-25). If salvation depended on us we would surely be lost, however, since our salvation depends on GOD keeping HIS promise to those who believe, we have the greatest of all possible guarantees.

In Mark 10:27, JESUS responded to HIS Disciples' question of "Who then can be saved?" There JESUS answered by saying, "With men it is impossible, but not so with GOD: for with GOD, all things are possible". There JESUS is saying, in effect, that, if a man is to depend upon his own efforts to achieve salvation, then, it is impossible for anyone. Salvation is a gift from GOD, and with GOD, all things are possible. If a man is to rely upon his own efforts, he can never be "saved". However, if he will rely on the saving power and redeeming love of GOD, then, he will be able to enter, for free, into the Kingdom of Heaven. That's the thought that JESUS stated then, and that's the thought that Paul is stating here in this letter to the Romans, and that's the thought that is still today, the very foundation of the Christian Faith.

Paul used Abraham as an example, because the Jews regarded him as the father of their race, and the earthly pattern of what a man should live like. Paul was seeking to prove that, what makes a man righteous, is not his works, but rather, it is his faith and trust in GOD. Paul also used Abraham as an example, because, he himself, was a wise teacher who could discern human thoughts. He recognized that faith is abstract, and, that the human mind finds it very difficult to grasp abstract ideas.

Using Abraham as an example was Paul's way of personifying faith, and thereby, developing a better understanding of what is needed, if we are to please GOD. We must, in our human minds, receive and accept by faith, the divine and abstract ideas of GOD, WHO HIMSELF is Spirit (abstract), and dwells in Heaven. To trust and believe GOD is necessary, not just for the people in Paul's day, nor, just for the Jews, but rather, for all people, for all time.

PERSONAL APPLICATION:

(1). Guard against losing faith in GOD because, you are disappointed by people.
(2). Christians cannot operate without faith, and we certainly can't please GOD without it.
(3). Abraham is the personification of faith in Paul's illustration, because he lived before there was a Ten Commandments. Through faith only, he believed in, and obeyed GOD, and GOD, as a result, accredited him with righteousness, and he received salvation based on his faith.
(4). When we obey GOD, we can be assured that GOD will keep HIS word of promise to us even today, because GOD cannot and will not change.

LIFE RESPONSE:

Pray a prayer of thanks to GOD for promises kept, when we trust and believe on HIM. Thank HIM for life more abundant, when we live it through CHRIST JESUS,

WHO continues to fulfill those promises that enhance and enrich our lives each day that we follow HIM.

KEY VERSE: Romans 4:20-21

DEVOTIONAL PASSAGES: Genesis 15:12-20, Acts 13:26-41, John 14:1-3

CHRIST DIED FOR US
(CHRIST provides courage to endure)

SCRIPTURE:
The King James Version
(Romans 5:1-11 & 18-21)

5 **(1)** Therefore being justified by faith, we have peace with GOD through our LORD JESUS CHRIST: **(2)** By WHOM also we have access by faith into this grace wherein we stand, and rejoice in hope of the glory of GOD. **(3)** And not only so, but we glory in tribulations also: knowing that tribulation worketh patience; **(4)** And patience, experience; and experience, hope: **(5)** And hope maketh not ashamed; because the love of GOD is shed abroad in our hearts by the HOLY GHOST which is given unto us. **(6)** For when we were yet without strength, in due time CHRIST died for the ungodly. **(7)** For scarcely for a righteous man will one die: yet peradventure for a good man some would even dare to die. **(8)** But GOD commendeth HIS love toward us, in that, while we were yet sinners, CHRIST died for us. **(9)** Much more then, being now justified by HIS blood, we shall be saved from wrath through HIM. **(10)** For if, when we were enemies, we were reconciled to GOD by the death of HIS SON, much more, being reconciled, we shall be saved by HIS life. **(11)** And not only so, but we also joy in GOD through our LORD JESUS CHRIST, by WHOM we have now received the atonement. **(18)** Therefore as by the offence of one judgment came upon all men to condemnation; even so by the righteousness of ONE the free gift came upon all men unto justification of life. **(19)** For as by one man's disobedience many were made sinners, so by the obedience of ONE shall many be made righteous. **(20)** Moreover the Law entered, that the offence might abound. But where sin abounded, grace did much more abound: **(21)** That as sin hath reigned unto death, even so might grace reign through righteousness unto eternal life by JESUS CHRIST our LORD.

COMMENTARY:

The sin of Adam brought physical death. The Resurrection of CHRIST brought spiritual life. Because one man disobeyed GOD, many people became sinners

(Romans 5:12). However, because one other MAN obeyed GOD, many people will be made right in GOD's sight (Romans 5:17).

In the original Greek, the word Paul uses for "access", in Romans 5:2, is "prosagoge" (pros-a-gogue-ay), and it means "to introduce, or usher someone else into the presence of royalty". It can also be defined as "a safe haven, or harbor". We have "access" to GOD through our faith in JESUS CHRIST, WHO came into the World, and overcame the World, by way of HIS enduring SPIRIT. We can now rejoice in our trials because we know that those trials are not meant to make us fail, but rather, they are tests, that are meant to strengthen us, and make us better warriors in the army of CHRIST. Trials help us learn to endure, and endurance develops strength and character. Our character then strengthens our hope and confidence in the gift of salvation (Romans 5:2-4).

In John 15:13 JESUS says that, "greater love hath no man than this, that a man lay down his life for his friends" (KJV). This gives us confidence in salvation, because, here JESUS is saying in effect, that, from that glorious moment when HE died on the cross at Golgotha, we were no longer just HIS servants, but, at that moment, we became HIS friends. By the sin of Adam, all men became sinners and were alienated from GOD. In total contrast, by the righteousness of CHRIST, all men can become righteous, and can be restored into a right relationship with GOD (Romans 5:18).

Paul says it more clearly in 1 Corinthians 15:21-22 where he states, "For since by man came death, by MAN came also, the resurrection of the dead. For in Adam all die, even so in CHRIST shall all be made alive" (KJV). There are two basic Jewish ideas that come into play when reading this passage. One is "solidarity". The Jews never really thought of themselves as individuals, but rather, they were a part of a chosen clan, a family, or a nation, and whatever happened to one, happened to all. The other thing that comes into play is that, at least in those days, death was considered to be the direct consequence, or result, of sin. The Jews believed that sin was intimately connected with death, and in essence, they are right.

GOD's love, however, is not limited to just a select few, and HE proved that when HE extended HIS love to the entire ungodly human race by sending HIS SON JESUS to die on the cross for our iniquities. And since HIS death brought reconciliation to us all, while we were still HIS enemies, we are now reconciled, and should have confidence that HIS sacrifice will complete the work of salvation in us (Romans 5:6-11).

GOD's law was given to us so that all people could see how sinful they are. The more people sin, the more abundantly GOD's wonderful grace and kindness will manifest itself. And just as sin had previously ruled over all people, bringing them to death, so now GOD's grace and kindness rules instead, giving us right standing with HIMSELF, and resulting in eternal life through CHRIST JESUS, our LORD (Romans 5:20-21).

Through faith in CHRIST, we can see an ultimate happy ending to the unpleasant circumstances that we now find ourselves in. Faith gives us hope to see beyond our suffering, tribulation, and understanding. Faith enables us to realize how GOD can work a greater good in our lives through difficult times. And we can also rejoice and come to rest in the hope of a glorious future that was prepared for us long ago, by a kind and loving GOD.

PERSONAL APPLICATION:

(1). Think of someone, whom you know, who may be seeing themselves as being in a hopeless situation because of a recent setback in life. Then, try and come up with some GODLY ways in which you might be able to encourage them in the SPIRIT of hope which CHRIST JESUS lends to us as Christians.

(2). Arm them with a list of scriptures, perhaps from this lesson that may seem most appropriate to their struggle.

(3). When a person has hope, they also have peace, and that is true with everyone. Through the power of CHRIST we can be conquerors of all things, even the things that bring us harm and disappointment in this world.

LIFE RESPONSE:

Pray a prayer of thanks to GOD for giving us hope, through JESUS CHRIST, our LORD and SAVIOR, WHO then sent to us, the HOLY SPIRIT, to empower us to do the same for others.

KEY VERSE: Romans 5:5

DEVOTIONAL PASSAGES: Philippians 4:6-7, Psalms 40:1-3, Psalms 34:17-19

LESSON SEVEN:

SIN'S POWER IS BROKEN
(We have a new life in CHRIST)

SCRIPTURE:
The King James Version
(Romans 6:1-14)

6 **(1)** What shall we say then? Shall we continue in sin, that grace may abound? **(2)** GOD forbid. How shall we, that are dead to sin, live any longer therein? **(3)** Know ye not, that so many of us as were baptized into JESUS CHRIST were baptized into HIS death? **(4)** Therefore we are buried with HIM by baptism into death: that like as CHRIST was raised up from the dead by the glory of the FATHER, even so we also should walk in newness of life. **(5)** For if we have been planted together in the likeness of HIS death, we shall be also in the likeness of HIS resurrection: **(6)** Knowing this, that our old man is crucified with HIM, that the body of sin might be destroyed, that henceforth we should not serve sin. **(7)** For he that is dead is freed from sin. **(8)** Now if we be dead with CHRIST, we believe that we shall also live with HIM: **(9)** Knowing that CHRIST being raised from the dead dieth no more; death hath no more dominion over HIM. **(10)** For in that HE died, HE died unto sin once: but in that HE liveth, HE liveth unto GOD. **(11)** Likewise reckon ye also yourselves to be dead indeed unto sin, but alive unto GOD through JESUS CHRIST our LORD. **(12)** Let not sin therefore reign in your mortal body, that ye should obey it in the lusts thereof. **(13)** Neither yield ye your members as instruments of unrighteousness unto sin: but yield yourselves unto GOD, as those that are alive from the dead, and your members as instruments of righteousness unto GOD. **(14)** For sin shall not have dominion over you: for ye are not under the Law, but under Grace.

COMMENTARY:

When we were joined to CHRIST in "spiritual baptism", we became so united with HIM that HIS death became our death to sin. Sin no longer has dominion over our lives, and we are free to make the choice of obeying GOD fully. JESUS' resurrection became our resurrection and we now share in HIS new life. In sharing in that new life, we are now able to live for GOD, just as CHRIST does (Romans 6:1-11).

In the Greek, the word used for "truth" is "aletheia" (al-ay-thi-a), and it means "in harmony with reality". When we come to CHRIST, we experience a "spiritual reality" or "truth" through faith, that, we otherwise, would have never known. We have chosen to live in harmony with reality, and can now, consider ourselves to be dead to the world of sin, and new citizens to the "kingdom of Heaven". We must now allow the Laws of GOD to become paramount to us in our new life, and we are ready to accept the reality of GOD's truth, based on faith in HIS WORD. We are saying to GOD that we no longer want to be slaves to sin, but rather, we choose to be servants to HIM, through HIS grace (Romans 6:12-14).

Chapter 6 of Paul's letter to the Romans is all about "present tense salvation". It exemplifies the truth that we are being perpetually saved by CHRIST JESUS daily, and in fact, moment by moment. And even though our propensity to sin remains with us, and indeed, we all still feel our "sin nature" tugging at us, however, now, we have the strength of CHRIST, through GOD's infusion of the HOLY SPIRIT, to help us win those battles between our "reason to do right", and our natural "passion to want to do wrong".

PERSONAL APPLICATION:

(1). Make the choice of "Life in CHRIST". It is an option that is readily available to you, as long as you have breath in your body.

(2). If you are a professed Christian, you must remain constantly in the word of GOD. Every time you begin to release your grip on the word of GOD, the old life begins to regain its grip on you. Spend as much time in GOD's word as you possibly can.

(3). From the very moment you close your bible and put it down, you begin the process of being untrained all over again, so don't wait long before you pick it up again.

LIFE RESPONSE:

Pray and ask GOD daily how you can remain out of the grip of your personal sins against HIM. Pray that HE continue HIS work in you, by releasing those strongholds that have dominated your life for so long, and then, help you to help others, through your experiences.

KEY VERSE: Romans 6:4

DEVOTIONAL PASSAGES: 1 Corinthians 12:12-13, 1 Corinthians 15, John 20:1-10

LESSON EIGHT:

GOD'S LAW REVEALS OUR SINS
(GOD's Law only serves to show us how far we are from HIS standards)

SCRIPTURE:
The King James Version
(Romans 7:1-13)

7 **(1)** Know ye not, brethren, (for I speak to them that know the Law,) how that the Law hath dominion over a man as long as he liveth? **(2)** For the woman which hath an husband is bound by the Law to her husband so long as he liveth; but if the husband be dead, she is loosed from the Law of her husband. **(3)** So then if, while her husband liveth, she be married to another man, she shall be called an adulteress: but if her husband be dead, she is free from the Law; so that she is no adulteress, though she be married to another man. **(4)** Wherefore, my brethren, ye also are become dead to the Law by the body of CHRIST; that ye should be married to another, even to HIM WHO is raised from the dead, that we should bring forth fruit unto GOD. **(5)** For when we were in the flesh, the motions of sins, which were by the Law, did work in our members to bring forth fruit unto death. **(6)** But now we are delivered from the Law, that being dead werein we were held; that we should serve in newness of spirit, and not in the oldness of the letter. **(7)** What shall we say then? Is the Law sin? GOD forbid. Nay, I had not known sin, but by the Law: for I had not known lust, except the Law had said, "Thou shalt not covet". **(8)** But sin, taking occasion by the commandment, wrought in me all manner of concupiscence. For without the Law sin was dead. **(9)** For I was alive without the Law once: but when the commandment came, sin revived, and I died. **(10)** And the commandment, which was ordained to life, I found to be unto death. **(11)** For sin, taking occasion by the commandment, deceived me, and by it slew me. **(12)** Wherefore the Law is holy, and the commandment holy, and just, and good. **(13)** Was then that which is good made death unto me? GOD forbid. But sin, that it might appear sin, working death in me by that which is good; that sin by the commandment might become exceeding sinful.

COMMENTARY:

After Paul had finished arguing how "Law" and "Faith" are incompatible in principal, he moves on to show how a believer can be legally free from obligation to the Law, and, why it is also necessary and essential. In the Greek, the word Paul uses here for "law" is "nomos" (nom-os), which means, "law through the idea of prescriptive usage". In other words, it is to be used only when it applies to a given situation, even though it is always, in principle, the law.

In this particular passage, the law represents the Old Testament revelation of standards that are regarded as "righteous behavior" by GOD. Rarely has Paul written a more complex passage than the one we see here. Its basic thought is rooted in the old adage that "death cancels all contracts". In Romans chapter 7, verses 2-3, Paul uses the example of how a woman, who is married, is only bound to her husband for as long as he is alive. After he dies, she is free to remarry without being guilty of adultery according to the Law, and is thereby freed from the law that once bound her to him.

In the same way, Paul says, we as Christians are no longer bound by the law, because we, in effect, died to its power when we died with CHRIST on the cross, or, in other words, when we became Christian believers. We are now united with CHRIST, the ONE WHO was raised from the dead, and we can now serve GOD fully, not in the old way, by obeying the letter of the law, but rather, in the new way of CHRIST JESUS, which is by the HOLY SPIRIT (Romans 7:4-6).

Paul also wants his readers to be clear on one other thing, and that is that, the law itself is not sinful, but rather, it was given to us to show us how sinful we are. We would never have known that adultery, or murder, or lying, or stealing, or coveting, or any other thing that is wrong was wrong, had GOD not given us HIS Law to reveal it to us (Romans 7:7).

The Law itself is divine, because it is the very voice of GOD speaking to us. In fact, it is holy and just, and it is designed by GOD, for our greater good. And so, the Law creates sin only in the sense that it defines and identifies sin to us. Some people are frightened by the idea that we, as Christians, have no obligation to keep GOD's Law per say. And here in this passage, Paul shows how we are actually freed from such obligations, because CHRIST has already died for all of our sins, past, present, and future. HE died for all mankind in general, and all Christians, in particular.

GOD now calls for us to form a new relationship with HIM, through CHRIST JESUS, by way of the HOLY SPIRIT in us. And so, we see that freedom from the Law, does not promote sin, but rather, it promotes righteousness, and a desire to obey the Law of GOD at all times (Romans 7:8-13).

PERSONAL APPLICATION:

(1). As Christians, our focus must be on worshiping GOD in spirit and truth, not in law. Our worship in spirit and truth will compel us to desire to obey the Laws of GOD.

(2). When we were controlled by our old "sin nature" our sinful desires were aroused by the Law, and thereby, produced evil deeds. The death of CHRIST released us from the bondage of sin, and thereto, released us from the Law. Now we are free to obey GOD in spirit and in truth, by being CHRIST-like in our behavior.

(3). To be like CHRIST, calls for us to learn WHO CHRIST is, through Scripture.

LIFE RESPONSE:

Pray to GOD to give you completeness of understanding of this very complex scripture. Pray for HIS guidance, through the HOLY SPIRIT to be in control of your sin nature, through your power in CHRIST JESUS at all times, so that you may serve HIM better, through your life's examples.

KEY VERSE: Romans 7:4

DEVOTIONAL PASSAGES: Matthew 25:31-46, Mark 2:23-28, John 4:23-24

STRUGGLING WITH SIN
(The sinfulness of sin)

SCRIPTURE:
The King James Version
(Romans 7:14-25)

7 (14) For we know that the Law is spiritual: but I am carnal, sold under sin. **(15)** For that which I do I allow not: for what I would, that do I not; but what I hate, that do I. **(16)** If then I do that which I would not, I consent unto the Law that it is good.

(17) Now then it is no more I that do it, but sin that dwelleth in me. **(18)** For I know that in me (that is, in my flesh,) dwelleth no good thing: for to will is present with me; but how to perform that which is good I find not. **(19)** For the good that I would I do not: but the evil which I would not, that I do. **(20)** Now if I do that I would not, it is no more I that do it, but sin that dwelleth in me. **(21)** I find then a law, that, when I would do good, evil is present with me. **(22)** For I delight in the Law of GOD after the inward man: **(23)** But I see another law in my members, warring against the Law in my mind, and bringing me into captivity to the law of sin which is in my members. **(24)** O wretched man that I am! Who shall deliver me from the body of this death? **(25)** I thank GOD through JESUS CHRIST our LORD. So then with the mind I myself serve the Law of GOD; but with the flesh the law of sin.

COMMENTARY:

In the biblical Greek, the word used to describe "sin nature" is, "epithumia" (ep-ee-thoo-mee-ah), and "it is that battle that rages on inside of each of us, between the "reason" to do what is right, and the "passion" to want to do what is wrong". Human nature is so corrupted by sin that we cannot respond favorably to GOD in our own power. We need the power of the HOLY SPIRIT within us to be able to win the battle against our own sinful nature, and be able to respond to GOD in a positive way.

In Romans 7:14-25, Paul reveals to us in the most vivid of pictures, the truth about the struggles that are contained in this first act of the "human drama", which is our life right now, here on earth. Before we come to CHRIST, and receive the infusion of the HOLY SPIRIT, our "reason" and "passion" comes from the same source, which is our "sinful nature" within. We can't possibly win in our struggle with sin, because our desire to sin isn't going to counter itself. It can only agree with itself, and therefore, more often than not, when we have to make the decision between doing what is right, and doing what is wrong, too often we choose to do what is wrong. In fact, we can sometimes even lose sight of what the right thing to do is, altogether.

We even begin to use our "human ingenuity" to justify our wrong with an attitude of indifference, convincing ourselves that there is no right or wrong, and, that we should do what makes us happy. We end up living in an unstructured existence that has no boundaries, and we can care less who we hurt, physically, or emotionally, in the process.

But when we receive the power of the HOLY SPIRIT, HE becomes our power of reasoning, and as a result, our reasoning, and our passion no longer comes from the same source. We then have a GODly sense of influence, or "reasoning" to combat our human sin nature, or "passion".

Here in this passage, Paul is writing about his own experiences as a believer, and it undoubtedly parallels the experiences of all believers, then and now. We are in a constant struggle to do right, but seem to fail again and again, even after we first become Christians. It is only as we mature in the faith, that, we seem to get a grip on our inner struggles with sin, and begin to become more and more like CHRIST in our thinking and behavior. We, through the power of the HOLY SPIRIT, develop a conscience for when we are about to move out of the Will of GOD, and we can thereby "repent", or have a "change of mind" (while still in the thinking stages of sin) before we sin, not after.

As Paul writes in verse 14, GOD's Law is, and has always been good, and, it will always continue to be good. The trouble is not with the law, but rather, it is with us, as we have been sold into the slavery of sin since the Garden of Eden, and sin has remained as our master, throughout the generations.

Because of Adam and Eve's disobedience to GOD in the Garden of Eden, man had fallen out of a relationship of friendship with GOD. Most of the time, we know perfectly well when we are doing wrong, but, we do it anyway, because it agrees with our natural desire to sin (Romans 7:16-17). It took the life of CHRIST to restore that lost relationship of friendship with GOD. CHRIST JESUS' obedience to GOD in the "Garden of Gethsemane" offset Adam and Eve's disobedience to GOD, in the "Garden of Eden".

Since GOD offers forgiveness of sin, through CHRIST JESUS' sacrifice at Golgotha, we are no longer under the bondage of sin. CHRIST has already died to pay the sacrificial price for all of man's sins, past, present, and future, and we no longer have to be slaves to our desires to transgress against GOD, and indeed, against our own bodies. Now, we are free to serve GOD, because we now live in the SPIRIT, and walk in the newness of life, that is, CHRIST JESUS, our LORD.

PERSONAL APPLICATION:

(1). If you are dying to find a new way to live, only an introduction to JESUS will help. JESUS is the only ONE, WHO knows what is wrong, and the only ONE, WHO can set things right. You can find HIM in the word of GOD.
(2). When we read the word of GOD, and study and meditate on it, our inadequacies are revealed to us, little by little.
(3). Most people will agree that it is a struggle to do the right thing much of the time, even though we really want to. Our only hope is to stop struggling, and turn our lives over to CHRIST, and accept the fact that, we as humans cannot live a life of joy, apart from GOD.

LIFE RESPONSE:

Pray for continued strength, through CHRIST JESUS, that you can learn to hear and obey the prompting of the HOLY SPIRIT more clearly, and have the strength and courage to change your mind, about sinning, before you sin, from this day forward.

KEY VERSES: 7:24-25a

DEVOTIONAL PASSAGES: Isaiah 59:1-2, Matthew 5:27-30, John 8:1-11

GOD'S GLORY REVEALED
(GOD works for the good of those who love HIM)

SCRIPTURE:
The King James Version
(Romans 8:18-39)

8 **(18)** For I reckon that the sufferings of this present time are not worthy to be compared with the glory which shall be revealed in us. **(19)** For the earnest expectation of the creature waiteth for the manifestation of the sons of GOD. **(20)** For the creature was made subject to vanity, not willingly, but by reason of HIM WHO hath subjected the same in hope, **(21)** Because the creature itself also shall be delivered from the bondage of corruption into the glorious liberty of the children of GOD. **(22)** For we know that the whole creation groaneth and travaileth in pain together until now. **(23)** And not only they, but ourselves also, which have the first fruits of the spirit, even we ourselves groan within ourselves, waiting for the adoption, to wit, the redemption of our body. **(24)** For we are saved by hope: but hope that is seen is not hope: for what a man seeth, why doth he yet hope for? **(25)** But if we hope for that we see not, then do we with patience wait for it. **(26)** Likewise the SPIRIT also helpeth our infirmities: for we know not what we should pray for as we ought: but the SPIRIT ITSELF maketh intercession for us with groanings which cannot be uttered. **(27)** And HE that searcheth the hearts knoweth what is the mind of the SPIRIT, because HE maketh intercession for the saints according to the will of GOD. **(28)** And we know that all things work together for good to them that love GOD, to them who are the called according to HIS purpose. **(29)** For whom HE did foreknow, HE also did predestinate to be conformed to the image of HIS SON, that HE might be the FIRSTBORN among many brethren. **(30)** Moreover whom HE did predestinate, them HE also called: and whom HE called , them HE also justified: and whom HE justified, them HE also glorified. **(31)** What shall we then say to these things? If GOD be for us, who can be against us? **(32)** HE that spared not HIS OWN SON, but delivered HIM up for us all, how shall HE not with HIM also freely give us all things? **(33)** Who shall lay any thing to the charge of GOD's elect? It is GOD that justifieth. **(34)** Who is HE that condemneth? It is CHRIST that died, yea rather, that is risen again, WHO is even at the right hand of GOD, WHO also maketh intercession for us. **(35)** Who shall separate us from the love of CHRIST? Shall tribulation, or distress, or persecution, or famine, or nakedness, or peril, or sword? (36) As it is written, for THY sake we are killed all day long; we are accounted as sheep for the slaughter. (37) Nay, in all these things we are more than conquerors through HIM that loved us. (38) For I am persuaded, that neither death, nor life, nor angels, nor principalities, nor powers, nor things present, nor things to come, (39) Nor height, nor depth, nor any other creature, shall be able to separate us from the love of GOD, which is in CHRIST JESUS our LORD.

COMMENTARY:

The Christian Hope is invincible, because it is founded in GOD. Peace, hope, patience, comfort, and love are the things that men, such as Paul, recognized in GOD. Here in Paul's letter to the Romans, as it is expressed in chapter 8 verse 19, in his original Greek writings, Paul uses a wonderful word for "earnest expectation" or "hope for the future". It is "apokaradokia" (a-pock-a-rah-do-KEE-ah), and it describes the attitude of a man, who scans the horizon, with his head thrust forward, as he eagerly anticipates the first signs of the coming of the glory of GOD.

You see, for Paul, life was not an overbearing and defeated waiting, but rather, it was a throbbing and very vivid expectation. The Christian has always been, is now, and will forever be, a part of the "human experience". By that I mean, from within, we must all suffer with our own "sin nature", in the Greek, "epithumia" (ep-i-thoo-mee-ah), that war we wage within ourselves between "reason" and "passion". And from the outside, we must all live in a world full of death and decay, as we continue to suffer the consequences of the sins of others.

But, thanks to GOD, as Christians, we do not just live in the world. As Christians, we also live in JESUS CHRIST. Therefore, we do not see only the world, but we must look beyond this world, to GOD. That way, we do not just see the consequences of ours, and other people's sin, we're also able to see the power and mercy of GOD's love. And so we see that the essence to the Christian Faith must always be hope, and never despair. The true Christian isn't waiting for death, but rather, we wait for life. The true Christian, just like Paul, must always wait, in "apokaradokia".

GOD does not want us to wallow in the troubles and failures of this life. HE wants us to always, through our strength in CHRIST JESUS, be able to look beyond this world to a future with HIM. We need to know that HIS power and love will always be able to overpower all of the worries and issues of this life. And, we can finally come to rest in the thought, that this life is not the final act of the human drama, when we truly have faith, and trust in GOD. As Christians, we know that all things work together for good, to those who love GOD (Romans 8:28), but when trouble comes, we're sometimes hard pressed to recall it. Paul was convinced that nothing could separate him from the love and safety found in GOD (Romans 8:38-39), and we, if we are truly believers, should be convinced of that too.

PERSONAL APPLICATION:

(1). Try to recall a time in your life when GOD has worked out a situation for your good, when you could only see the bad.

(2). Now think of a time when you went ahead and tried to work something out in your own strength, and after failing, realized that you should have prayed first, and then, waited on GOD to work it out, through HIS strength.

(3). Suffering and hardship does not mean that we've been abandoned by GOD, nor are we ever separated from HIS love. No matter what happens to Christians in this life, GOD forever holds us firmly in HIS mighty hands.

LIFE RESPONSE:

Write down on a piece of paper, what you believe to be currently, your biggest problems. Then go to GOD in prayer over those problems, or situations, and ask GOD to remove them from your life if it be HIS will. And if it's not HIS will, pray that HE give you the strength to endure in suffering for the faith you have in HIM that HE will work things out for the greater good, in the end.

KEY VERSE: Romans 8:28

DEVOTIONAL PASSAGES: Isaiah 26:3-4, Psalm 40:1-3, Philippians 4:6-7

LESSON ELEVEN:

(34)

JESUS IS THE ROCK OF OUR SALVATION
(But HE is a stumbling block to those without belief)

SCRIPTURE:
The King James Version
(Romans 9:30-33)

9 (30) What shall we say then? That the Gentiles, which followed not after righteousness, have attained to righteousness, even the righteousness which is of faith. (31) But Israel, which followed after the Law of righteousness, hath not attained to the Law of righteousness. (32) Wherefore? Because they sought it not by faith, but as it were by the works of the Law. For they stumbled at the stumblingstone; (33) As it is written, behold, I lay in Sion a stumblingstone and rock of offence: and whosoever believeth on HIM shall not be ashamed.

COMMENTARY:

If a man's heart goes out in love and submission to JESUS, then JESUS represents for that man, salvation. But if a man's heart is entirely unmoved or angrily rebellious, JESUS represents for that man, condemnation". In Romans 9:30-33, the Apostle Paul once again hits his readers with the, now familiar, rhetorical question, "What then shall we say?"

Here, Paul draws a stunningly vivid contrast between the Jewish way, and the Gentile way, of viewing GOD. The Jews set out to try and earn their way to Heaven through deeds, and, by trying to follow the letter of the Law, while the newly admitted Gentiles in the church, tended to seek GOD the correct way, which is of course, by faith.

When we try to earn our way to heaven the way the Jews sought to do, we are, in effect, attempting to put GOD into our debts. But man, because of his imperfections, can never satisfy the letter of the Law. He can never walk according to the light of GOD, he can only seek to walk in the light of CHRIST. And even that can't be done without the power of the HOLY SPIRIT in him to guide and counsel him in the right direction.

We can never stack up enough brownie points, that GOD will owe us salvation in return for our good deeds. Salvation is the gift that keeps on giving through faith, and it cannot be purchased by money, or, by deeds. JESUS CHRIST never did conform to the Jews' expectations from HIM, and as a result, they rejected HIM rather than to respond to HIM by faith. They ultimately delivered HIM into the hands of Pilate, and in order to save himself from his own, self-imposed, troubled career, Pilate was compelled, to sentence CHRIST to death.

Driven by their hatred for JESUS, the Jewish leaders lost all sense of proportion, and totally forgot about the mercy, that they had so often preached about in the temple. They forgot all justice, and in the end, as it is recorded in John 19:15, they denounced GOD, and professed Caesar as their king.

And to show how GOD had anticipated this kind of action from HIS "chosen people", Paul reminds them of a couple of contrasting quotes from the prophet Isaiah, some 750 years earlier (Isaiah 8:14 & 28:16), in verse 33. Here, we are forced to accept one great eternal truth about CHRIST JESUS. HE was sent into this world to be both a SAVIOR of men, and, the TOUCHSTONE by which all men are judged.

PERSONAL APPLICATION:

(1). GOD shows mercy to anyone HE chooses, and HE does not show favoritism based on race, creed, color, money, or deeds. If you seek to win GOD's favor, it must be done by having faith in HIM only. You must turn yourself over to GOD, and be inwardly certain that HE will see you through and provide for all of your needs.

(2). Remember, GOD chose Jacob over Esau before either one of them had done anything good, or bad, because scripture tells us that GOD made this choice while they were still in the womb of Rebekah (Genesis 25:23).

(3). Just as any man, who creates something, has a right to do with that creation, what he pleases, so can GOD do the same with us, HIS creation. And GOD directs HIS favor towards those, who have undying faith in HIM, and HE selects Christians, from both, the Jews, and the Gentiles.

LIFE RESPONSE:

Pray and ask GOD to help you to increase your faith in HIM, through HIS OWN ways, and give you the strength to endure those tests. GOD already knows the areas in which you are weak, and so, just ask HIM to expose and remove anything from your life that might weaken your trust and faith in HIM.

KEY VERSE: Romans 9:33

DEVOTIONAL PASSAGES: Genesis 25:23, Isaiah 28:16, Romans 9:15

PROCLAIMING THE GOSPEL
(Spreading the Gospel by word and deed)

SCRIPTURE:
The King James Version
(Romans 10:1-17)

10 (1) Brethren, my heart's desire and prayer to GOD for Israel is, that they might be saved. (2) For I bear them record that they have a zeal of GOD, but not according to knowledge. (3) For they being ignorant of GOD's righteousness, and going about to establish their own righteousness, have not submitted themselves unto the righteousness of GOD. (4) For CHRIST is the end of the Law for righteousness to every one that believeth. (5) For Moses describeth the righteousness which is of the Law, "That the man which doeth those things shall live by them". (6) But the righteousness which is of faith speaketh on this wise, "Say not in thine heart, who shall ascend into Heaven?" (that is, to bring CHRIST down from above:) (7) Or, "Who shall descend into the deep?" (that is , to bring up CHRIST again from the dead.) (8) But what saith it? The word is nigh thee, even in thy mouth, and in thy heart: that is, the word of faith, which we preach; (9) That if thou shalt confess with thy mouth the LORD JESUS, and shalt believe in thine heart that GOD hath raised HIM from the dead, thou shalt be saved. (10) For with the heart man believeth unto righteousness; and with the mouth confession is made unto salvation. (11) For the scripture saith, "Whosoever believeth on HIM shall not be ashamed". (12) For there is no difference between the Jew and the Greek: for the same LORD over all is rich unto all that call upon HIM. (13) "For whosoever shall call upon the name of the LORD shall be saved". (14) How then shall they call on HIM in WHOM they have not believed? And how shall they believe in HIM of WHOM they have not heard? And how shall they hear without a preacher? (15) And how shall they preach, except they be sent? As it is written, "How beautiful are the feet of them that preach the gospel of peace, and bring glad tidings of good things!" (16) But they have not all obeyed the gospel. For Esaias saith, "LORD, who has believed our report?" (17) So then faith cometh by hearing, and hearing by the word of GOD.

COMMENTARY:

The reason why the gospel has to be preached is because men continue to suppress the truth. In the Greek, the word used for "truth" is "aletheia" (al-ay-thi-a), and it is "that which is in harmony with reality". The truth is, that JESUS has accomplished the whole purpose of the Law, and that all, who believe in HIM are made right with GOD. And that is the gospel, the good news, or "truth", that must be preached by all who follow JESUS.

The "good news" of JESUS CHRIST, or "the Gospel" comes from the Greek word "euangelizo" (yoo-angghel-id-zo), and it describes, not only the message, but it also describes the act of preaching the message. Out of the 76 times the word "gospel" is used in the New Testament, 60 of those occurrences are in the Apostle Paul's letters. We must all, in some way, "evangelize" the gospel of CHRIST, especially if we are, in any sense, going to proclaim ourselves to be HIS followers.

Paul has already shown us how righteousness has always been a gracious gift from GOD in chapter 9. Now, his argument shifts to how GOD continues to be loyal to us with HIS Covenant promises. HE has not rejected us, but rather, we have rejected HIM. Paul acknowledged the Jews enthusiasm for GOD, but, because they did not accept CHRIST, their zeal was misdirected, and as a result of rejecting CHRIST, they also, unwittingly, rejected GOD (Vs. 1-4).

The Jews steadfastly tried to earn their way to Heaven by following the letter of the Law, but Paul reasoned that the only way of getting right with GOD, was through faith in JESUS CHRIST. Salvation will always come only by trusting CHRIST, through the message that is preached by HIS servants, and that way, JESUS can always be in the reach of those who seek HIM. And when we confess with our mouths, we activate GOD's angels around us, who then begin to protect from the angels of satan. That then gives us time to fill our hearts with love for CHRIST, through understanding GOD's word, which is the gospel, with the help and guidance of the HOLY SPIRIT.

Anyone who believes in CHRIST, and enters into a personal relationship with HIM, will not be disappointed, and it does not matter if you are Jew, or Gentile. But our "personal relationship" with CHRIST must be "publicly personal" as well as "privately personal".

We must be willing to display an outward expression of our love and belief in CHRIST JESUS, WHO ushered in to us, salvation. And our commitment to CHRIST must be exemplified in both our "public and "private" lives, and, in no uncertain terms.

Everyone is on equal footing as far as GOD is concerned, because we are all sinners, and we are all called to believe, in order to be saved. We don't have to be able to write, or think, like the apostle John, nor do we need to be able to travel all over the world, and preach like the Apostle Paul. We just have to be willing to talk about the good news we know about CHRIST to those, who we come in contact with everyday. People need to hear the "Word", before they can believe the "Word", therefore, if you have the "Word", you are obligated by CHRIST, to share the word, with everyone that you meet.

All Christians are "called" by GOD to fulfill the great "Divine Commission of CHRIST", as it is recorded in Matthew 28:19-20. "Go ye therefore, and teach all nations, baptizing them in the name of the FATHER, and of the SON, and of the HOLY GHOST: Teaching them to observe all things whatsoever I have commanded you: and, lo, I am with you alway, even unto the end of the world. Amen.

PERSONAL APPLICATION:

(1). Let your mouth express the love you have for CHRIST in your heart.
(2). Start ministering for CHRIST in your home, neighborhood, and workplace, through your behavior.
(3). Keep in mind that your greatest witnessing will be, in the way you, yourself, behave publicly and privately, and not necessarily, in what you say.

LIFE RESPONSE:

Pray and give thanks to GOD for the Good News of CHRIST JESUS. Express to HIM that your heart is ready to use those gifts and talents that HE has given you to help bring others to CHRIST.

KEY VERSES: Romans 10:14-15

DEVOTIONAL PASSAGES: 1 John 1, John 1:1-5, Acts 2:14-21

LESSON THIRTEEN:

GOD'S MERCY IS FOR EVERYONE
(GOD is merciful to all people)

SCRIPTURE:
The King James Version
(Romans 11:25-36)

11(25) For I would not, brethren, that ye be ignorant of this mystery, lest ye should be wise in your own conceits; that blindness in part is happened to Israel, until the fullness of the Gentiles be come in. **(26)** And so all Israel shall be saved: as it is written, "There shall come out of Sion the DELIVERER, and shall turn away ungodliness from Jacob: **(27)** For this is MY covenant unto them, when I shall take away their sins". **(28)** As concerning the Gospel, they are enemies for your sake: but as touching the election, they are beloved for the FATHER's sakes. **(29)** For the gifts and calling of GOD are without repentance. **(30)** For as ye in times past have not believed GOD, yet have now obtained mercy through their unbelief: **(31)** Even so have these also now not believed, that through your mercy they also may obtain mercy. **(32)** For GOD hath concluded them all in unbelief, that HE might have mercy upon all. **(33)** O the depth of the riches both of the wisdom and knowledge of GOD! how unsearchable are HIS judgments, and HIS ways past finding out! **(34)** "For who hath known the mind of the LORD? Or who hath been HIS counsellor? **(35)** Or who hath first given to HIM, and it shall be recompensed unto HIM again?" **(36)** For of HIM, and through HIM, and to HIM, are all things: to WHOM be glory for ever. Amen.

COMMENTARY:

In Romans 11:25, the word the apostle Paul uses for "mystery", in his original Greek writings is, "musterion" (moos-tay-ree-on), and it is "a secret, through the idea of silence imposed by initiation into a religious rite". It is a technical theological term that New Testament writers use to indicate an aspect of GOD's eternal plan that was not revealed to the Old Testament prophets, with the exception of CHRIST JESUS.

In this particular passage, the mystery that was revealed is the unexpected salvation of the Gentiles as a result of the Jew's rejection of the good news of

CHRIST. However, this large conversion of Gentiles did not mean that GOD had reneged on the words of the Old Testament prophets. When the full number of Gentiles has been converted, history will then re-focus on Israel as the chosen people of GOD.

GOD's plan to put Israel aside temporarily, so that HE could show grace to the Gentiles, should not be cause for conceit on their part. It is simply another of GOD's plans to further magnify HIS OWN power and glory, and to further make HIS wishes known to us, that all men would choose salvation.

There still remains in this world, many Jews who are enemies of the Good News of JESUS CHRIST, and because of it, the Gentiles stand to benefit greatly. However, GOD cannot, and will not ever, withdraw the promise that HE made to Abraham, Isaac, and Jacob, no matter how many members of the chosen nation withdraw from HIM.

All people are imprisoned by their own disobedience to GOD, and we all, because of it, need GOD's mercy. And so GOD sent a DELIVERER to Jerusalem one day, in the person of JESUS CHRIST, and by doing so, HE shared with the whole world, HIS wonderful and abounding grace.

Oh what a wonderful GOD we have, and, oh how impossible it is to understand HIS reasons, and HIS methods. All that we know for sure is that HE created everything, and everything that exists came from HIM. We also know that everything is intended to glorify HIS OWN divine and holy name, and, at long last, I've come to realize that, in the final analysis, it never has been the wrath of GOD that chases men so relentlessly, but rather, it is the love of GOD, for all mankind, that keeps HIM in hot pursuit of us.

PERSONAL APPLICATION:

(1). It is good to know that GOD is trustworthy, and that, he will never go back on HIS promises, to all mankind. And no matter how much man has sinned against HIM, HE remains loyal to us. And so the first application is to meditate on that Thought.

(2). Notice how GOD is both kind and severe. HE is kind to those who trust in HIS kindness, and severe to those who disobey, and betray HIS largesse.

(3). GOD does not show favor based on your race, but rather, HE shows favor to those who trust and obey HIM continuously. Set about learning to put your trust in GOD. HE is the only ONE who will never let you down.

LIFE RESPONSE:

Pray for a heart that is dedicated to GOD, forever.

KEY VERSE: Romans 11:33

DEVOTIONAL PASSAGES: 2 Samuel 24:14, Psalm 40:11, Psalm 89:1-2

LESSON FOURTEEN:

LIFE IN THE GOSPEL AS ONE BODY IN CHRIST
(Challenge the pattern of the world through a life in CHRIST)

SCRIPTURE:
The King James Version
(Romans 12:1-3 & 9-21)

12(1) I beseech you therefore, brethren, by the mercies of GOD, that ye present your bodies a living sacrifice, holy, acceptable unto GOD, which is your reasonable service. (2) And not be conformed to this world: but be ye transformed by the renewing of your mind, that ye may prove what is that good, and acceptable, and perfect, will of GOD. (3) For I say, through the grace given unto me, to every man that is among you, not to think of himself more highly than he ought to think; but to think soberly, according as GOD hath dealt to every man the measure of faith. (9) Let love be without dissimulation. Abhor that which is evil; cleave to that which is good. (10) Be kindly affectioned one to another with brotherly love; in honour preferring one another; (11) Not slothful in business; fervent in spirit; serving the LORD; (12) Rejoicing in hope; patient in tribulation; continuing instant in prayer; (13) Distributing to the necessity of saints; given to hospitality. (14) Bless them which persecute you: bless, and curse not. (15) Rejoice with them that do rejoice, and weep with them that weep. (16) Be of the same mind one toward another. Mind not high things, but condescend to men of low estate. Be not wise in your own conceits. (17) Recompense to no man evil for evil. Provide things honest in the sight of all men. (18) If it be possible, as much as lieth in you, live peaceably with all men. (19) Dearly beloved, avenge not yourselves, but rather give peace unto wrath: for it is written, vengeance is mind; "I will repay", saith the LORD. (20) "Therefore if thine enemy hunger, feed him; if he thirst, give him drink: for in so doing thou shalt heap coals of fire on his head". (21) Be not overcome of evil, but overcome evil with good.

COMMENTARY:

Romans chapter 12, along with 1 Corinthians 12, presents to us the Christian image of what the Holy Body of CHRIST, which is the Church, should look like. Paul has already shown how GOD has moved to provide and impart righteousness (chapters 6-8). Now he moves on to the more practical issues that go to the heart of Christian theology, and what the attitude of the true Christian should be like. CHRIST does not ask that we die for HIM. HE asks that we live for GOD. Paul says we should strive to be a living, acceptable, Holy sacrifice to GOD, and not allow ourselves to be conformed to the world, but rather, to be transformed from it.

As GOD's messenger, Paul warns us to be honest in our estimation of ourselves, by measuring our value by how much faith GOD has given us. And in doing so, we will be able to function better in the body of CHRIST. And just as our bodies have many parts that must work together in unison, so it is with the body of CHRIST, which is of course, the Church.

As Christians, we've all become a part of CHRIST's body and we each have different tasks to perform, but, at the same time, we all belong to each other, and, need each other. GOD has given each of us certain gifts, and we are obligated by GOD to use those gifts in service of HIM, and, each other. We are to genuinely love each other, honor each other, and love what is right, while enthusiastically serving GOD in the body of CHRIST, in our homes, and, in all other areas of our lives.

Do not curse those who trouble you, but rather, pray for them that GOD might bless them. When others are happy, be glad that they are happy, not envious because you're not. And, when they are sad, we should share with them, in their sorrow. Do your part to contribute to peace and don't try to repay people for their evil deeds toward you, for that is a matter for GOD to handle. Don't let evil conquer you, but rather, access the power of the HOLY SPIRIT in you, that you may be able to conquer evil.

GOD's righteousness is revealed through the transformed lives of men and women, who strive to reflect HIS image to others through their behavior. As a person is transformed in their mind, and is, as a result, made more like CHRIST, they begin to, not only approve of, but also desire GOD's will. To do GOD's Will, will become paramount to them, as they begin to discover and understand more and more, that which pleases GOD. What pleases GOD and what is good for us, are, in fact, one in the same thing. In that sense, which is the spiritual sense, a person becomes complete in every other way, and, is able to walk in the newness of life, that is CHRIST JESUS, and of course, enjoy GOD's Will full time.

The commands of Scripture are as real today, as they were in the beginning. GOD's, expectations of us, has not changed over time. HE still expects us to do things that the world cannot do, or understand. Things like, serving, instead of wanting to be served all the time, sharing, instead of keeping things to ourselves, blessing people, instead of cursing them, loving, instead of hating. All of these actions are conditions of the heart that are expressed in our lives on a daily basis. And they really do identify, just whose side we are really on. It is always a sad commentary to hear a non-believer say this about a Christian,

"You know, I didn't really notice anything different about that person. What makes being a Christian so special?"

PERSONAL APPLICATION:

(1). The first thing we must be willing to do to come to CHRIST is to leave the world. It is a requirement for the person who wishes to transform their life to look more like the SAVIOR.

(2). GOD does not desire change that comes through human self-sacrifice. HE desires a transformation, or metamorphosis that can only come through the empowerment of the HOLY SPIRIT.

(3). Write down a list of changes you already know you need to make, and then, set about putting those changes into effect using what you've learned about GOD's holy standards as your guide.

(4). When you encounter people, habits, or patterns of behavior that are contrary to your new commitment to CHRIST, have the courage to quickly disassociate yourself from them.

LIFE RESPONSE:

Pray to GOD for courage to no longer be fascinated with the idea, or desire to blend in with the world. Pray that you can be a better witness for Christianity, to the world, through your daily behavior. Pray for the courage you need to reach out to the world in an effort to "feed JESUS' sheep" with the powerful, life-changing news of GOD's Holy Word.

KEY VERSE: Romans 12:2

DEVOTIONAL PASSAGES: James 1:19-27, James 2:1-13, James 3:1-12

RESPECT FOR AUTHORITY
(Pay all your debts, except the debt of love for others)

SCRIPTURE:
The King James Version
(Romans 13)

13(1) **Let every soul be subject unto the higher powers. For there is no power but of GOD: the powers that be are ordained of GOD. (2) Whosoever therefore resisteth the power, resisteth the ordinance of GOD: and they that resist shall receive to themselves damnation. (3) For rulers are not a terror to good works, but to the evil. Wilt thou then not be afraid of the power? Do that which is good, and thou shalt have praise of the same: (4) For he is the minister of GOD to thee for good. But if thou do that which is evil, be afraid; for he beareth not the sword in vain: for he is the minister of GOD, a revenger to execute wrath upon him that doeth evil. (5) Wherefore ye must needs be subject, not only for wrath, but also for conscience sake. (6) For this cause pay ye tribute also: for they are GOD's ministers, attending continually upon this very thing. (7) Render therefore to all their dues: tribute to whom tribute is due; custom to whom custom; fear to whom fear; honour to whom honour. (8) Owe no man any thing, but to love one another: for he that loveth another hath fulfilled the law. (9) For this, thou shalt not commit adultery, thou shalt not kill, thou shalt not steal, thou shalt not bear false witness, thou shalt not covet; and if there be any other commandment, it is briefly comprehended in this saying, namely, thou shalt love thy neighbour as thyself. (10) Love worketh no ill to his neighbour: therefore love is fulfilling of the Law. (11) And that, knowing the time, that now it is high time to awake out of sleep: for now is our salvation nearer than when we believed. (12) The night is far spent, the day is at hand: let us therefore cast off the works of darkness, and let us put on the armour of light. (13) Let us walk honestly, as in the day; not in rioting and drunkenness, not in chambering and wantonness, not in strife and envying. (14) But put ye on the LORD JESUS CHRIST, and make not provision for the flesh, to fulfil the lusts thereof.**

COMMENTARY:

All the governments of man are servants of GOD, but few recognize it in the conscience sense. Governments are used and manipulated by GOD to achieve HIS purposes, weather they know it or not. Human governments must, at least, enforce a minimum amount of justice, lest that government be in danger of collapsing on itself. If criminal behavior were allowed to go unchecked, human society would come to an abrupt and tragic halt.

In Romans 13, the apostle Paul lectures on obedience to the authority that GOD has vested in mankind. Out of respect and reverence for GOD, a Christian must show respect for the governing body of any particular city, state, or country, in which they reside. We must pay our taxes and obey the laws of that society at all times (Romans 13:1-6).

At first sight, this passage tends to provoke a surprising reaction from most Christians because it seems to suggest absolute obedience on the part of a Christian to conform to civil law. However, it is a commandment that also shows up a few other times in New Testament scripture, notably, 1 Timothy 2:1-2, Titus 3:1, 1 Peter 2:13-17.

I suppose one could debate that these passages were written during a time before the Roman government had begun to persecute Christians. However, we know for a fact that, in the book of Acts, often the secular magistrate served as a safe haven for those same Christians who were attacked by their Jewish brothers for preaching the doctrine of CHRIST. And even centuries later, long after persecutions had begun, during the reign of the Emperor Claudius (Acts 18), the Christian teachers still stuck to this philosophy. It was this persistent, consistent teaching that continued even when those persecutions escalated during the reign of the Emperor Nero, when both Paul and Peter were reported to have been martyred.

We can see quite vividly how the unchanging Word of GOD prevailed in strong Christian hearts down through the ages, even when it seemed unbearably difficult to obey HIS commands. Paul saw rebellion and insurrection against governments as a direct negation of Christian principals and doctrine. Paul correctly saw that no one can completely separate themselves from the society in which they live.

Everyone enjoys certain benefits from being a part of an organized government. And everyone has a responsibility to dedicate a part of themselves to the safety and welfare of their respective municipality, state, and nation. For instance, we should all pay our taxes, because our taxes supplies the need of those who work in government functions such as the military, law enforcement, fire fighting, garbage pick-ups, etc. (Romans 13:6-7).

Paying our debts is something that all of us struggle with from time to time, but in order to satisfy and fulfill GOD's requirement, we must all try and make sure we eventually get our debts paid. In fact, Paul says that the only debt that we should leave owing is "the debt of love for each other as Christians". That is a debt, Paul says, that we should never finish paying. If we continue to love our neighbor, we will continue to fulfill the requirement of GOD's Law (Romans 13:8).

The commandments against adultery, murder, stealing, coveting, etc. are all summed up in the commandment, "Love your neighbor as yourself". If you love your neighbor, you won't commit adultery with their spouse. If you love your neighbor, you won't kill them, or steal from them, or despise them with envy of what they have, or own (Romans 13:9-10).

The end of all things is near, for each of us, personally. For, that is the warning that the ancient prophets, and New Testament writers and thinkers all leave us with. And that is the warning that Paul gives us here in this passage starting in verse 11. Because our time here on earth is short, that gives us greater reason to want to do that which is right in the eyes of GOD. It is time to shed our evil ways like dirty clothes, and then, re-dress ourselves in the armor of right living. We must become decent and true in everything that we do so that our behavior will be accepted by both man and GOD (Romans 13:11-13a).

The days of wild partying, getting high, engaging in all sorts of immoral living, and fighting with each other because of jealous and envious motives, must end, especially among those who profess to be Christians (Romans 13:13b). Just as Christians are a part of the body of CHRIST's Church, they are, just as well, a part of the body of their nation, and should serve as a GODly example, or "light", to the world at large.

In this world, and, in the world to come, there can be no such thing as an isolated individual. Paul clearly understood GOD's intent in secular governments and he also clearly understood GOD's intent in the Church as well. He clearly and correctly saw, both the Church, and the secular nation, as instruments in the hands of GOD, both unwittingly poised for a time when GOD would choose to awaken them for use in HIS OWN grand and divine plan. GOD always has a way of showing us that HE is subject to no one's will but HIS OWN. And we might as well come to rest in that thought, lest we continue to be disappointed in our position in a world that only GOD, can, and will, control.

PERSONAL APPLICATION:

(1). The only debt GOD wants us to owe is the debt of love for one another, and that is a debt, which can never be paid. Our continued love for each other enables us to fulfill the Law of GOD, and that, will raise your credit score to the heights of Heaven.

(2). There is never a right time to do the wrong thing, and there is never a wrong time to do the right thing.

(3). Christians must submit to governing authorities, because they are servants of GOD's put in place to lead us (although, most often, unwittingly). And so, submission, to authorities, shows reverence for GOD indirectly.

LIFE RESPONSE:

Pray to GOD for the strength of submission, so that you may be able to clothe yourself in the love of CHRIST, rather than gratify yourself with the desires of a sinful nature.

KEY VERSE: Romans 13:1

DEVOTIONAL PASSAGES: Matthew 22:17-21, Ephesians 6:1-3, Ephesians 6:12

LESSON SIXTEEN:

THE DANGER OF CRITICISM
(Don't make life hard for another Christian)

SCRIPTURE:
The King James Version
(Romans 14)

14 (1) Him that is weak in the faith receive ye, but not to doubtful disputations. (2) For one believeth that he may eat all things: another, who is weak, eateth herbs. (3) Let not him that eateth despise him that eateth not; and let not him which eateth not judge him that eateth: for GOD hath received him. (4) Who art thou that judgest another man's servant? To his own master he standeth or falleth. Yea, he shall be holden up: for GOD is able to make him stand. (5) One man esteemeth one day above another: another esteemeth every day alike. Let every man be fully persuaded in his own mind. (6) He that regardeth the day, regardeth it unto the LORD; and he that regardeth not the day, to the LORD he doth not regard it. He that eateth, eateth to the LORD, for he giveth GOD thanks; and he that eateth not, to the LORD he eateth not, and giveth GOD thanks. (7) For none of us liveth to himself, and no man dieth to himself. (8) For whether we live, we live unto the LORD; and whether we die, we die unto the LORD: whether we live therefore, or die, we are the LORD's. (9) For to this end CHRIST both died, and rose, and revived, that HE might be LORD both of the dead and living. (10) But why dost thou judge thy brother? Or why dost thou set at nought thy brother? For we shall all stand before the judgment seat of CHRIST. (11) For it is written, as I live, saith the LORD, every knee shall bow to me, and every tongue shall confess to GOD. (12) So then every one of us shall give account of himself to GOD. (13) Let us not therefore judge one another any more: but judge this rather, that no man put a stumbling block or an occasion to fall in his brother's way. (14) I know, and am persuaded by the LORD JESUS, that there is nothing unclean of itself: but to him that esteemeth any thing to be unclean, to him it is unclean. (15) But if thy brother be grieved with thy meat, now walkest thou not charitably. Destroy not him with thy meat, for whom CHRIST died. (16) Let not then your good be evil spoken of: (17) For the kingdom of GOD is not meat and drink; but righteousness, and peace, and joy in the HOLY GHOST. (18) For he that in these things serveth CHRIST is acceptable to GOD, and approved of men. (19) Let us therefore follow after the things which make for peace, and things wherewith one may edify another. (20) For meat destroy not the work of GOD. All things indeed are pure; but it is evil for that man who eateth with offence. (21) It is good neither to eat flesh, nor to drink wine, nor any thing whereby thy brother stumbleth, of is offended, or is made weak. (22) Hast thou faith? Have it to thyself before GOD. Happy is he that condemneth not himself in that thing which he alloweth. (23) And he that doubteth is damned if he eat, because he eateth not of faith: for whatsoever is not of faith is sin.

COMMENTARY:

In Romans 14, the Apostle Paul once again turns his attention to the subject of "faith-based righteousness" in regards to relationships within the Christian community. We, as believers, are to accept one another without condemning each other for our personal convictions regarding our interpretations about our Christian faith.

We, as human beings, have no right to judge others in that respect, because, in all respects, we are all indeed, people under judgment. We are all responsible to the LORD, so let HIM tell others, through the HOLY SPIRIT, whether they are right or wrong. The LORD's OWN power will convict them, and help guide them in their decisions to do the right thing. In other words, each person will have a personal conviction about all matters of the heart (Vs. 3-4).

Christians come to the faith from various backgrounds and we all grow spiritually at different rates. If we are to live in the Christian community in the harmony of CHRIST, we must all learn to avoid differences of opinion over matters that are not sin according to Scripture. For example, a believer with certain Christian principles should not be invited into the Christian community with the intentions of changing their view or opinion about things that do not go against Christian doctrine, by debating with them.

Here in this chapter, Paul uses as an example, one of the most debated areas of Christian principles, which is the subject of food consumption. One man's Christian faith allows him to eat everything, while another man's faith only allows him to eat vegetables (v. 2). In such situations, Paul says, neither believer should judge the other's motives. A Christian servant's motives for doing things should only be judged by GOD, and not by his fellow believers, especially regarding those things that are not forbidden by Scripture (Vs. 4).

Another area Paul touches on is, the days of which a person worships. One person may consider one day more important, or more sacred than the other, while another person may hold that they are all equally important. Paul says that each person should be convinced in his own mind, examining his own heart to be sure that he is doing what he feels the LORD would have him do. That person should then, hold his opinion up to the LORD, and this is true regarding all issues where an honest difference of opinion exists between Christians (Vs. 5-6).

Everyone in life, and in death, is under the watchful eye of GOD, and we are all accountable to HIM, and not to each other, at least, not for our motives behind our actions regarding things that are not prohibited by Scripture. One Christian should not look down on another Christian because of the things that they do, that are not specifically prohibited by GOD. It is GOD's job to dole out "krino" (judgment), and you can be assured that every one of us will have to make an account for the deeds done in our lifetimes (Vs 7-12).

Paul's warnings against judging relates specifically to the Christian's attitudes and actions, toward the convictions of other Christians, especially regarding their respective Christian beliefs. We should not cause another Christian to stumble, by arguing over things, and trying to get that person to commit to certain convictions that are not of scripture, but rather, are just a matter of opinion. Paul says that he is perfectly sure, on the authority of CHRIST JESUS, that no food, in and of itself, is wrong to eat. But if someone believes it is wrong, then, for that person, it is wrong, and as Christian brothers and sisters, we should respect that, as it is (Vs. 13-14).

The kingdom of GOD is not a matter of what we eat or drink, but rather, it is a matter of living a life of goodness, peace, and joy, in the HOLY SPIRIT. Our aim should always be toward harmony and trying to build each other up in the Church. We should never tear apart the work of CHRIST over what a person eats or drinks, nor, over what days of the week that person worships on. However, it is wrong to eat or drink something, or do anything when, if by eating, or by doing it, it causes another Christian to stumble. But we should never condemn ourselves for something that we know is all right by Scripture (Vs. 13-22), and if you harbor any doubts about something you may be doing, then don't do it, lest you be condemned for not acting in faith. If you do anything that you believe is not right, you are sinning. For whatsoever is not of faith, is sin (v. 23).

PERSONAL APPLICATION:

(1). Try to discover ways to identify and avoid the stumbling blocks that Christians often create between themselves, in the Christian community.
(2). Think of some people in your church that you know are burdened by heavy

issues, yet no one has made an effort to uplift them, then, commit yourself to reaching out to them.

(3). Make a pledge that you will not build new stumbling blocks for other Christians by criticizing, gossiping, stereotyping, etc., and then, sign your name to that pledge.

LIFE RESPONSE:

Pray and ask GOD to open your spiritual eyes so that you may see the stumbling blocks that we may be putting before other Christians by your own behavior. Pray also that HE allow the SPIRIT to work inside of you and help you to honor others and not judge others wrongly.

KEY VERSE: Romans 14:13

DEVOTIONAL PASSAGES: Mathew 6:14, Matthew 7:12, Matthew 25:31-46

LESSON SEVENTEEN:

LIVING TO PLEASE OTHERS
(CHRIST didn't live to please HIMSELF, so, why should we?)

SCRIPTURE:
The King James Version
(Romans 15:1-13)

15 (1) We then that are strong ought to bear the infirmities of the weak, and not to please ourselves. (2) Let every one of us please his neighbour for his good to edification. (3) For even CHRIST pleased not HIMSELF; but, as it is written, "The reproaches of them that reproached thee fell ME". (4) For whatsoever things were written aforetime were written for our learning, that we through patience and comfort of the Scriptures might have hope. (5) Now the GOD of patience and consolation grant you to be like-minded one toward another according to CHRIST JESUS: (6) That ye may with one mind and one mouth glorify GOD, even the FATHER of our LORD JESUS CHRIST. (7) Wherefore receive ye one another, as CHRIST also received us to the glory of GOD. (8) Now I say that JESUS CHRIST was a minister of the circumcision for the truth of GOD, to confirm the promises made unto the fathers: (9) And that the Gentiles might glorify GOD for HIS mercy; as it is written, "For this cause I will confess to THEE among the Gentiles, and sing unto THY name". (10) And again HE saith, "Rejoice, ye Gentiles, with HIS people". (11) And again, "Praise the LORD, all ye Gentiles; and laud HIM, all ye people. (12) And again, Esaias saith, "There shall be a ROOT of Jesse, and HE shall rise to reign over the Gentiles; in HIM shall the Gentiles trust". (13) Now the GOD of hope fill you with all joy and peace in believing, that ye may abound in hope, through the power of the HOLY GHOST.

COMMENTARY:

In Romans 15:1-13, Paul expands on the subject that he had already introduced in chapter 14, of living to please others. Our pursuit of righteous living requires us to be able to live a life of love for one another. It means that we must be able to stop judging others, and, at the same time, evaluate how the exercising of our personal freedoms may affect other people's lives. The strong Christian must be able to tolerate the weak Christian in the interest of building them up.

Paul had already written in chapter 14 how Christians should not condemn, despise, or hinder the conduct of one another. Here in chapter 15, he gives us another principal that we need to observe, while dealing with one another, and that is, that, we must strive to be "imitators" of CHRIST. We must be aware at all times that JESUS was a person WHO always ministered on behalf of others, and as Christians, we need to reflect that image to the world, through our own behavior.

As Paul continues to define the responsibilities of Christians towards one another, he also gives us a wonderful summary of what should characterize, or be the attributes of, the Christian community as a whole. Paul's idea of a Christian community, is that of a place, where everyone has a strong consideration for the needs of others. It should also be a place that identifies itself by being encouraged by the study of the Scriptures, and, by a desire to incorporate GOD's word into the everyday lives of its people.

The Christian community should also have a fortitude that is exemplified in the attitude that each individual has towards life, and how they are able to cope with life, in a GODly manner. It is a community that needs to represent to the world, the personification of hope. We should be able to exist in harmony with one another, because, the "CHRIST" in us, is greater than the "world" in us. And finally, we must be in the "Praise Mode", at all times remembering just WHO we represent in the world, and that is of course, CHRIST JESUS.

After pointing to CHRIST as a model for all Christians, Paul moves on to talk a bit more about JESUS' ministry and the objectives thereof. First of all, JESUS came to us as a servant. GOD had two objectives to accomplish through JESUS' mission. The first was to confirm the promise of the Patriarchs, Abraham, Isaac, Jacob, and David, for the Jews, and the second was so that the Gentiles may also glorify HIM for HIS mercy.

Those two purposes are now being achieved as Israel, as a nation, has been set aside, and the church is being formed with both Jews and Gentiles all over the world. This will be fulfilled in the future when Israel, once again, will take its place as head of the nations of the earth, and become a blessing to all people. To demonstrate the validity of this claim, Paul goes on to cite four Old Testament passages (read Romans 15:9-12). The significance of these quotations is that they are taken, one from each division of the Old Testament, the Law (Moses), the Prophets (Isaiah), and the Psalms (King David).

There is a progression of thought in these four quotations that we'll do well not to miss. In the first quotation, David praises GOD among the Gentiles. In the second, Moses exhorts the Gentiles to rejoice with the Jews. In the third, the psalmist commands the Gentiles to praise the LORD. And, in the fourth, Isaiah predicts that the Gentiles will live under the rule of the MESSIAH, and will find hope in HIM. Our peace results from the assurance that GOD will fulfill all of our hopes. And Paul's desire was that GOD would fill his readers with the joy and peace that would reign eternal. Only when the surge of CHRIST's power fills the voids of our human weaknesses, will we, ourselves, be able to overcome this life, just as CHRIST did.

PERSONAL APPLICATION:

(1). Be responsible to CHRIST JESUS for your conscience, and don't attempt to make others responsible for you.

(2). JESUS helped us to establish a pattern of welcome, that we must, in turn, convey to others all along our Christian walk.

(3). The strong Christian is obligated to take the initiative in the Christian community, and, in the world. They must consider, at all times, what is most helpful in building up the weak.

(4). Show love and concern by actively reaching out to embrace the weak. That way you will be able to build a spirit of unity in the Christian congregation.

LIFE RESPONSE:

Pray for continued strength through CHRIST JESUS. The farther you go along your Christian struggle, the more you need prayer, not less. Amen.

KEY VERSE: Romans 15:7

DEVOTIONAL PASSAGES: 1 Corinthians 3:15-20, 1 Corinthians 12:12-27, 1 Corinthians 13

PAUL'S REASON FOR WRITING
Romans 15:14-22

15 (14) And I myself also am persuaded of you, my brethren, that ye also are full of goodness, filled with all knowledge, able also to admonish one another. (15) Nevertheless, brethren, I have written the more boldly unto you in some sort, as putting you in mind, because of the grace that is given to me of GOD. (16) That I should be the minister of JESUS CHRIST to the Gentiles, ministering the Gospel of GOD, that the offering up of the Gentiles might be acceptable, being sanctified by the HOLY GHOST. (17) I have therefore whereof I may glory through JESUS CHRIST in those things which pertain to GOD. (18) For I will not dare to speak of any of those things which CHRIST hath not wrought by me, to make the Gentiles obedient, by word and deed, (19) Through mighty signs and wonders, by the power of the SPIRIT of GOD; so that from Jerusalem, and round about unto Illyricum, I have fully preached the gospel of CHRIST. (20) Yea, so have I strived to preach the gospel, not where CHRIST was named, lest I should build upon another man's foundation: (21) But as it is written, "To whom HE was not spoken of, they shall see: and they that have not heard shall understand". (22) For which cause also I have been much hindered from coming to you.

COMMENTARY:

Perhaps in this particular passage we get a clearer picture of the character of the man who spearheaded the Christian movement in the first century, than anywhere else, in any of his other letters. Here the Apostle Paul brings his dictations to his associate, Tertius, to an end as he shares with us, his reasons for writing to the Church at Rome. He says he writes to them, with a certain boldness and purpose, to really remind the Church at Rome of something that they already knew. It was GOD's grace that made him the servant of CHRIST to the Gentiles. Here Paul reveals himself as a man of "tact", as he assures the Church that they have what it takes to render an outstanding service to each other, and, to the LORD.

Paul had always shown himself to be more interested in what a person can be, than what a person was. He could see a person's faults clearly and he knew how to deal with them expertly, and, he claimed no glory for himself. He also wanted to send the important message that true Christians must live to please others. Paul brought his message of CHRIST JESUS to the Gentiles, and he led them to CHRIST with that message, and, by the way he himself lived. He says his ambition was to preach the Good News wherever the name of JESUS CHRIST had never been heard, as opposed to teaching it were someone else had already gotten the Church started. And that ambition that was provided by the HOLY SPIRIT eventually propelled Paul to preach the Word all over the world, as they knew it at that time.

PERSONAL APLICATION:

(1). Try viewing people for what they can be in CHRIST, not for what they are in the world.
(2). Try and practice an unselfish behavior instead of always focusing on yourself.
(3). Learn about CHRIST, and then, share what you've learned everywhere you go.

LIFE RESPONSE:

Pray to GOD for an unselfish lifestyle

KEY VERSES:

Romans 15:20-21

DEVOTIONAL PASSAGES: Psalm 101, Joshua 24:15

LESSON NINETEEN:

PAUL'S TRAVEL PLANS
Romans 15:23-33

15 **(23)** But now having no more place in these parts, and having a great desire these many years to come unto you; **(24)** Whensoever I take my journey into Spain, I will come to you: for I trust to see you in my journey, and to be brought on my way thitherward by you, if first I be somewhat filled with your company. **(25)** But now I go into Jerusalem to minister unto the saints. **(26)** For it has pleased them of Macedonia and Achaia to make a certain contribution for the poor saints which are at Jerusalem. **(27)** It hath pleased them verily; and their debtors they are. For if the Gentiles have been made partakers of their spiritual things, their duty is also to minister unto them in carnal things. **(28)** When therefore I have performed this, and have sealed to them this fruit, I will come by you into Spain. **(29)** And I am sure that, when I come unto you, I shall come in the fullness of the blessing of the Gospel of CHRIST. **(30)** Now I beseech you, brethren, for the LORD JESUS CHRIST's sake, and for the love of the SPIRIT, that ye strive together with me in your prayers to GOD for me; **(31)** That I may be delivered from them that do not believe in Judaea; and that my service which I have for Jerusalem may be accepted of the saints; **(32)** That I may come unto you with joy by the Will of GOD, and may with you be refreshed. **(33)** Now the GOD of peace be with you all. Amen.

COMMENTARY:

Here we see in this passage, Paul's plans for yet a third missionary journey. It would be his last. Actually, here Paul is speaking of both, an immediate plan, one that would take him to Jerusalem to deliver donations to the Church there, as they had been experiencing a famine at that time, and, of a future plan to travel to Spain, and to Rome to visit the Christians there.

Spain was an exciting place to be in those days as some of the greatest men of that era, such as Lucan, the great epic poet, Quintilian, perhaps the greatest teacher of oratory during that time, and Seneca, the great philosopher and the Prime Minister of Rome under Nero, where all Spaniards.

Spain also rested at the very western-most end of the civilized world at that time, and Paul was probably thinking how great it would be if he could evangelize Spain. It would be a tremendous boost for Christianity in that part of the world, and he could envision many great things springing up from there to help spread the gospel of CHRIST even more aggressively.

Whether or not Paul ever got to visit Spain, no one really knows for sure. We know for a certainty, however, that when he went to Jerusalem he was arrested and apparently spent the next four years in jail in Caesarea (two years), and, in Rome (two years under house arrest), and so it is unlikely that he did. We know also that, despite all of the predicaments that he'd find himself in, he was always planning ahead with great anticipation, while, at one and the same time, still remaining flexible. Wherever Paul went, he went with the confidence and knowledge of the full blessings of GOD, and he was proud of the fact that he would be able to share those blessings with the Christian saints of his day, wherever, and whenever he did arrive.

And finally, Paul always recognized the importance of intercessory prayer (Vs. 30-33), and here we also see him requesting prayer from the saints for himself. He wished for other believers to join him in his struggles through prayer, because he believed strongly that intercessory prayer was an effective means by which all believers could share in the ministries of others, without physically being there.

In this passage, Paul makes a specific request for prayer that he would be rescued from the unbelievers in Judea, and also, that his service in Jerusalem would be acceptable to the believers who lived there. Paul was acutely aware of the problems that he would face in Jerusalem (Acts 20:23), and he was deeply concerned, that, the offering that he was delivering from the Gentile Christians, would be distributed properly. If so, he would then be able to rest and relax among the saints, knowing that his job had been well done.

PERSONAL APPLICATION:

(1). Be responsible to CHRIST JESUS for your conscience, and don't attempt to make others responsible for you.

(2). JESUS helped us to establish a pattern of welcome, that we must, in turn, convey to others all along our Christian walk.

(3). The strong Christian is obligated to take the initiative in the Christian community, and, in the world. They must consider, at all times, what is most helpful in building up the weak.

(4). Show love and concern by actively reaching out to embrace the weak. That way you will be able to build a spirit of unity in the Christian congregation.

LIFE RESPONSE:

Pray for continued strength through CHRIST JESUS. The farther you go along your Christian struggle, the more you need prayer, not less. Amen.

KEY VERSE: Romans 15:30

LESSON TWENTY:

FINAL INSTRUCTIONS
(Division and obstacles)

SCRIPTURE:
The King James Version
(Romans 16:17-27)

16 **(17)** Now I beseech you, brethren, mark them which cause divisions and offences contrary to the doctrine which ye have learned; and avoid them. **(18)** For they that are such serve not our LORD JESUS CHRIST, but their own belly; and by good words and fair speeches deceive the hearts of the simple. **(19)** For your obedience is come abroad unto all men. I am glad therefore on your behalf: but yet I would have you wise unto that which is good, and simple concerning evil. **(20)** And the GOD of peace shall bruise satan under your feet shortly. The grace of our LORD JESUS CHRIST be with you. amen. **(21)** Timotheus my workfellow, and Lucius, and Jason, and Sosipater, my kinsman, salute you. **(22)** I Tertius, who wrote this epistle, salute you in the LORD. **(23)** Gaius mine host, and of the whole church, saluteth you. Erastus the chamberlain of the city saluteth you, and Quartus a brother. **(24)** The grace of our LORD JESUS CHRIST be with you all. Amen. **(25)** Now to HIM that is of power to stablish you according to my gospel, and the preaching of JESUS CHRIST, according to the revelation of the mystery, which was kept secret since the world began, **(26)** But now is made manifest, and by the Scriptures of the prophets, according to the commandment of the everlasting GOD, made known to all nations for the obedience of faith: **(27)** To GOD only wise, be glory through JESUS CHRIST for ever. Amen.

COMMENTARY:

Before Paul closes his letter to the Romans, he makes one last appeal to the Christians of that city, as he urges them to keep themselves in the love of GOD. He gives them something to help them in their efforts, by warning them to stay away from those who cause dissention, by teaching those things that are contrary to the doctrine already introduced to them by he and those who truly represent CHRIST JESUS.

William E. Channing wrote in his essay "Means of promoting Christianity" that, "The first laborers do little more than teach those, who come after them, what to avoid, and how to labor more effectually than themselves". It has been the Christian Hope, throughout the history of the church, that it be able to serve as motivation to make life on earth conform more fully with the word of GOD, as it was presented to us by JESUS CHRIST, during HIS three-year ministry here on earth.

All the information that we have about CHRIST, and Christianity, comes to us, from those who actually saw HIS miracles performed, and, who actually heard HIM speak. It is because they wrote to encourage believers, rather than to satisfy historical curiosity, that this information oftentimes leaves more questions, than it does answers, particularly, in the minds of unbelievers.

No one has ever been able to harmonize all of this information into a completely satisfying chronological account. The main reason for that is that, these Holy Scriptures that we see, hold, and possess now, where not assembled by the "authors of GOD" who wrote them, but rather, where assembled later on, by second, third, and even fourth generation workers and developers of the early church.

As long as we keep in mind, that, the "original workers" of the early church, where those hand-picked apostles of JESUS CHRIST, we should be able to come to rest in our hearts, that the words of the bible, and the ways of CHRIST are one and the same. We will also believe to a point of knowing, that GOD THE FATHER is the CREATOR and SUSTIAINER of all of life, and that the power of the HOLY SPIRIT will help us to remain in the will of the TRIUNE GOD. And so, we must be aware of the dissention brought on by false teaching.

The "peace of GOD" is the "peace of action and victory" because it does not allow us to submit to the world, but rather, it allows us to overcome the world as we desire more and more to be like CHRIST. The overpowering message in this Book of Romans is that, through a righteousness that is imputed to us through our faith in CHRIST JESUS, GOD will do what HE said HE would do. Only GOD could do it for the people of the world of the first century, and only GOD can do it for us now. And now, to the GOD of peace, WHO raised up again our LORD and SAVIOR, JESUS CHRIST from the dead. And to HIM that is able to establish us according to HIS OWN WORD. Indeed, to the ONLY WISE GOD, our SAVIOR, through CHRIST JESUS be glory and majesty, dominion and power, both now and forever. Amen.

PERSONAL APPLICATION:

(1). There is no short-cut to knowing GOD, and the only way to know GOD is through the study of HIS word. Just as you can't fall in love with another person without first getting to know them, so too with GOD, knowing comes before loving. GOD knows us, and because of it, HE loves us and desires the best for us.

(2). Paul's way is still the best way for dealing with people of dissention. If you can't convert them, stay away from them.

(3). The way of "loving one another" was perfected by the small groups in the "House Churches" of the first century. Start up a family home bible study and then expand it by inviting your neighbors to participate.

LIFE RESPONSE:

Pray to GOD and ask HIM to assist you in building a community of love where you live. Pray for a love that is GOD-inspired to permeate your life and the lives around you, so that there may be no dissention among you.

KEY VERSE: Romans 16:25

DEVOTIONAL PASSAGES: 1 Corinthians 1:10-17, 1 Corinthians 13, Galatians 6:1-10

LESSON TWENTY ONE:

(65)

THE ROMANS ROAD TO SALVATION
(How to use your bible to lead a person to CHRIST)

SCRIPTURE:
The King James Version
(The Book of Romans)
(Matthew 28:18-20)

And JESUS came and spake unto them, saying, "All power is given unto me in Heaven and in Earth. Go ye therefore, and teach all nations, baptizing them in the name of the FATHER, and of the SON, and of the HOLY GHOST: Teaching them to observe all things whatsoever I have commanded you: and, lo, I am with you alway, even unto the end of the world". Amen. - Matthew 28:18-20

—

The first and foremost duty of the Christian is to lead people to CHRIST and present them with an opportunity to accept HIS gift of Salvation, first with their lips, so that they may later come to accept HIM in their hearts, through the study of GOD's word, and, through the power and guidance of the HOLY SPIRIT. The following exercise is incorporated in this book to enable you to do just that, and is known to serious Christians, quite simply, as the "Romans Road to Salvation".

(1). Start by letting the person you're leading, know that all mankind is on the same level, as far as who is good, and who is not.

WHO IS GOOD?

"As it is written, There is none righteous, no, not one:" – ROMANS 3:10

—

(2). Let them know that, clearly, we have sinned and the bible confirms it.

WHO HAS SINNED?

"For all have sinned, and come short of the glory of GOD;" - ROMANS 3:23

—

(3). Tell them where sin came from.

WHERE DID SIN COME FROM?

"Wherefore, as by one man sin entered into the world, and death by sin; and so death passed upon all men, for that all have sinned:" - ROMANS 5:12

–

(4). Tell them what sin costs us.

GOD'S PRICE ON SIN

"For the wages of sin is death; but the gift of GOD is eternal life through JESUS CHRIST our LORD." – ROMANS 6:23

–

(5). Let them know that the price of sin is paid.

WHO PAID THE PRICE?

"But GOD commendeth HIS love toward us, in that, while we were yet sinners, CHRIST died for us." – ROMANS 5:8

–

(6). Show them the only way out.

THE ONLY WAY OUT

"That if thou shalt confess with thy mouth the LORD JESUS, and shalt believe in thine heart that GOD hath raised HIM from the dead, thou shalt be saved. For with the heart man believeth unto righteousness; and with the mouth confession is made unto Salvation" – ROMANS 10:9-10

–

(7). If they now wish to give their life to CHRIST, have them repeat after you, this prayer, or a similarly effective prayer.

LORD JESUS, I need YOU.
I thank YOU for dying on the cross for my sins.
I do earnestly repent for my trespasses against YOU,
And I open up the door to my heart,
And invite YOU in, as my LORD and SAVIOR.
I thank YOU for forgiving my sins,
And then offering me Eternal Life.
I accept YOUR offer of Salvation,
And I want YOU to take control of the throne of my life,
And make me into the kind of person that YOU want me to be.
It is in YOUR precious name that I pray. Amen.

I urge you to become familiar with this application, as it is the most important lesson in this book. If a Christian does not know how to bring another person to CHRIST, he or she is not a complete Christian. If a Christian knows this application, and yet, does not use it to save others, GOD will not hold you blameless for your fellowman's demise. Take heed and keep yourself in the love of GOD. Amen.

A FINAL LOOK AT THE LAW
(The LORD on Mount Sinai)

SCRIPTURE:
The King James Version
(Exodus 20:1-17)

20 (1) And GOD spake all these words saying, (2) I AM the LORD thy GOD, which have brought thee out of the land of Egypt, out of the house of bondage. (3) Thou shalt have no other Gods before ME. (4) Thou shalt not make unto thee any graven image, or any likeness of any thing that is in Heaven above, or that is in the Earth beneath, or that is in the water under the Earth: (5) Thou shalt not bow down thyself to them, nor serve them: for I the LORD thy GOD AM a jealous GOD, visiting the iniquity of the fathers upon the children unto the third and fourth generation of them that hate ME; (6) And shewing mercy unto thousands of them that love ME, and keep MY commandments. (7) Thou shalt not take the name of the LORD thy GOD in vain; for the LORD will not hold him guiltless that taketh HIS name in vain. (8) Remember the Sabbath day, to keep it holy. (9) Six days shalt thou labour, and do all thy work: (10) But the seventh day is the Sabbath of the LORD thy GOD: in it thou shalt not do any work, thou, nor thy son, nor thy daughter, thy manservant, nor thy maidservant, nor thy cattle, nor thy stranger that is within thy gates: (11) For in six days the LORD made Heaven and Earth, the sea, and all that in them is, and rested the seventh day: wherefore the LORD blessed the Sabbath day, and hallowed it. (12) Honour thy father and thy mother: that thy days may be long upon the land which the LORD thy GOD giveth thee. (13) Thou shalt not kill. (14) Thou shalt not commit adultery. (15) Thou shalt not steal. (16) Thou shalt not bear false witness against thy neighbour. (17) Thou shalt not covet thy neighbour's house, thou shalt not covet thy neighbour's wife, nor his manservant, nor his maidservant, nor his ox, nor his ass, nor any thing that is thy neighbour's.

COMMENTARY:

Shortly after JESUS made HIS final triumphant entry into Jerusalem, and HE had cleared the Temple of the thieves and moneychangers, HE entered into a discussion with the Sadducees, a group of wealthy Jews who often argued that there was no resurrection after death, among other things (Mark 12:18-27). As they debated, one of the teachers of religious Law was standing nearby listening to the discussion. Realizing how well JESUS had handled HIMSELF during the debate, he decided to pose this question to our LORD and SAVIOR, "Which is the first commandment of all?"

The word "first" in this passage, translates from the Greek word "prote", which means "most important". In other words, he is asking JESUS, "Which is the most important commandment in the Decalogue?" JESUS responds by reciting, from part one, of what is known in Jewish tradition, as the "Shema" (Deuteronomy 6:4-9). It is something that was recited twice daily by devout Jews, and stresses the unity of GOD and the importance of loving GOD and HIS laws.

JESUS tells him that "The first of all commandments is, Hear, O Israel; The LORD our GOD is one LORD: And thou shalt love the LORD thy GOD with all thy heart, and with all thy soul, and with all thy mind, and with all thy strength: this is the first commandment". This statement made by JESUS, quite literally, encompasses the first four commandments of the Decalogue, which all together tells us that we must have reverence and love for the ALMIGHTY GOD, our CREATOR.

The second part of JESUS' response was this; "And the second is like, namely this, Thou shalt love thy neighbor as thyself". This statement by JESUS encompasses the final six commandments, which altogether means that we must love one another. All together the Ten Commandments teaches us that "Love is Loyalty" (verses 1-5), "Love is Faithfulness" (verse 6), "Love is trusting" (verse 7), "Love is reverence for GOD" (verses 8-11), and finally, "Love is something that we must all have for one another" (verses 12-17), and, by obeying these laws, we show GOD that we love HIM.

These commandments express GOD's perfect will for us, and how the GOD WHO made us in HIS OWN image, wishes us to live here on earth. And so we see, in Exodus 20:1-3 that "the GOD WHO made us in HIS OWN image" tells us that we should have no other Gods before HIM. Unfortunately, the reality is that we tell "the God that we make in our own image", that, our own personal desires will be the only exception.

In Exodus 20:4-6, "the GOD WHO made us in HIS OWN image" tells us, that, we shouldn't make unto ourselves any graven images and then bow down and worship them. We tell "the God we make in our own image" that the only exceptions will be our houses, cars, jobs, clothes, and any other possessions we deem most important in life.

In Exodus 20:7, "the GOD WHO made us in HIS OWN image" tells us not to use HIS name in vain. We tell "the God we make in our own image" that we should scratch that commandment altogether.

In Exodus 20:8-11, "the GOD WHO made us in HIS OWN image tells us not to work seven days a week, or seven consecutive days. HE allows us to work up to six days, but the seventh day we must not work, but rest and keep it holy. We tell "the God we make in our own image" that the only exceptions will be in those weeks when we have been bad stewards with our time, talents, and treasures, and fallen behind in our responsibilities at home, or at work, or, have to satisfy our greedy appetite for more things.

And because we can't be faithful to those first four commandments, we are rendered helpless to adhere to the other six. When we can't honor GOD, we certainly aren't going to think enough of our parents to honor them. Without reverence for GOD, there will always be murder among us. Man without GOD will always disrespect the body that GOD made in HIS OWN image, by committing adulterous acts. We will always steal that which belongs to another. And if we can do those things, why wouldn't we lie to cover them up, or accuse someone else so that they might take the fall for us.

All of the above violations of GOD's law can stem from envy, the final "Thou shalt not" in the Decalogue. Envy is distain for GOD's goodness to someone else, and neglect of GOD's goodness to us. It is simply "desire" coupled with "resentment". It causes a person to be sad when others rejoice, and rejoice when others are sad. If the above scenario describes you, then you, like many, many others got that way, by first creating "a God in your own image" that you would like to, or could easily serve.

Warren Wiersbe once wrote, "It is not a mark of wisdom to try and second-guess GOD, because HIS ways and thoughts are far beyond our comprehension. We make GOD after our own image and conclude that HE thinks and acts just as we do, and, of course, we are wrong".

In Isaiah 55, the LORD invites us, through Isaiah, to partake in the salvation that would be delivered to us by CHRIST JESUS, some 750 years later. Here in this prophetic passage of Scripture, GOD invites all mankind to come and drink of the life-saving gift of the New Covenant that was to be ushered in to us by HIS only begotten SON. By accepting the invite, a person is saying that they are willing to trust in, and rely on HIM for Salvation. They are also indicating that they agree to obey GOD's commandments, which will lead them to a higher standard of living.

The blessings, which GOD bestows upon us, are free, and without merit. We can't buy it, or earn it through good deeds. In this passage, the salvation that GOD speaks of is probably, both "spiritual redemption", and "physical deliverance". The everlasting covenant, as it was presented to David had both "physical" and "spiritual" benefits and meaning. In verse 3 of Isaiah 55, we see GOD reminding us of that eternal covenant with Israel's greatest king, where HE promised that his royal line would continue for ever.

We must remember that GOD's covenant for man was presented to us in three stages, the "Abrahamic" stage, the "Davidic" stage, and the final "greater stage" that was ushered into us by CHRIST. The word "covenant", in the biblical context is different from the way we see it in the secular world. Its secular meaning is one of an "equal agreement between two or more equal parties". However, in the biblical sense, it takes on the same definition as an "advisory will". With a will, one person draws up all the terms and the benefactors have no say in what those terms should be. They can either, accept, or reject those terms, and, cannot alter, add to, or take away, from the contents of that document. GOD's "will" for us has to be that way, because inferior man cannot come into an equal agreement with GOD. And just as GOD promised to keep HIS good hand on Abraham and David, HE so assures to do the same for those who come to HIM and remain in HIM, through faith.

It is not possible to abide with this New Covenant, while we continue to practice our evil ways and deeds. We must also banish from our minds any thoughts of doing what is wrong. We must be willing to transform our minds and hearts to the point where we are no longer fascinated by wrong things, and allowing those wrong things to have power over us.

As Christians, our relationship with GOD must become our greatest asset, not our jobs, houses, cars, people, and other modern-day idols we choose to put before GOD. When we put our faith in any thing other than GOD, disappointment is inevitable. Without faith in GOD, it is impossible to please GOD. For whatever we choose to make GOD in our own minds, we must remember that HIS thoughts are not our thoughts, and HIS ways are infinitely higher than ours.

GOD will accomplish all things that are in HIS will, weather we believe in HIM or not. GOD gives us HIS WORD, and down through the ages, HE has commissioned faithful men and women to deliver that WORD throughout the whole world. And HIS WORD will never return void, and will always accomplish that which it set out to do. The miracle of CHRIST JESUS has brought great honor to the LORD's name, and serves as an everlasting reminder of HIS great power and unconditional love.

PERSONAL APPLICATION:

Stay strong in the LORD!

CLOSING THOUGHTS

ALL WE NEED IS LOVE

Faith, Hope, and Love, are the three great enduring things. They are the spiritual elements that must be embodied in every person, who desires to be a true follower of CHRIST JESUS, and, who wishes to worship GOD, in spirit, and in truth. And of those three elements, "Love" is the greatest. In the Apostle Paul's first letter to the Corinthians, the segment we now know as chapter 13 is perhaps the best-known passage. It has come to be known, the world over, as the "Love Chapter".

In this, now famous passage, Paul, moves from explaining how to recognize "spiritual gifts", in the previous chapter, to how one can measure and express, his or her spirituality, in the "most excellent way". And that way, Paul insists, is by showing "Love", an element of quality so vital, that without it, not even the greatest of spiritual gifts, can enrich and enhance the lives of those, who possess them, or the lives of the people that they seek to help (1 Corinthians 13:1-3).

Paul clearly understood that "Love" is not just an abstract, philosophical idea, but rather, it is practical, and must be expressed in the everyday actions and attitudes of the believer (verses 4-7). Even the greatest of spiritual gifts are limited and distorted, by their own mortalities and imperfections. In other words, no spiritual gift lasts forever, but rather, they fade and deteriorate, in conjunction with the aging process of the human body (verses 8-12).

However, through it all, we can rely on our Faith, Hope, and love, which is, GOD personified, to sustain us. And "Love" is the greatest quality, because it, quite literally, is the foundation of the Christian Faith, and, life itself. Understanding that, we can see, quite vividly, why "Love" is the true measure a person's spirituality, and it also exemplifies the closeness of one's relationship with GOD.

Paul sought to make sure that we realize, quite readily, who, among us is truly spiritual. And the only way to do that was, by first, making sure we understood the true nature of love, and then, by presenting to us, the criteria, by which we can evaluate the spirituality of others. This is so we won't be duped into following the leadership and advice of false teachers.

Paul, quite simply, shows us in his own brilliant sort of way, the true "behavioral definition" of "Love". In this passage, Paul is saying that, any person, who is a spiritual representative of GOD, "acts like it", not just "talks like it". GOD is love, and when JESUS came to earth, HE clearly demonstrated that Love to us, and for us, time and time again. As a result, HE became "LOVE" personified, in the eyes of men, for all times. HE served to show us what "Love" is supposed to look like, as an integral part of the human, earthly experience, or, in other words, how we are to incorporate this "Love" into our everyday actions, attitudes, and indeed, into our existence.

And while it is true that perfection won't come to the Church until GOD's program for it is consummated with the "second coming" of our LORD and SAVIOR, JESUS CHRIST, and until then, a church is only perfect when no human being is in it, we as Christians can still, all reach a high level of maturity, by learning and becoming accustomed to practicing the immortal acts of Love, already exhibited to us, by CHRIST JESUS, during HIS first advent.

As for "Faith" and "Hope", they are merely manifestations of "Love", but because of it, they too, will endure forever. All, that we know now, is partial and incomplete, because we are yet, mere children in CHRIST. And when we are children, we are expected to act like children, just as, when we grow up, we are expected to put away childish things and behavior.

Before we come to know CHRIST, we've already long become accustomed to looking at ourselves, through an unclean mirror, and, as a result, we do not see ourselves, as we really are. The blood of CHRIST gives us something, by which we can use, to clean that mirror off, and begin seeing ourselves clearly, for the very first time.

We are then able to walk into the store of GOD, and pick us up a free bottle of "faith". And then, we can take it home and use it to spray some "hope" on that unclean mirror. And with "Love", we can wipe away the old life, and usher in the new. Then, and only then, will we be able to turn ourselves around, and begin heading in the right direction, in the newness of life, that is found only in CHRIST JESUS.

THE ULTIMATE HAPPY ENDING:

In Revelation 22:1-5, the Apostle John is given a few more facts by the angel of GOD, in his vision concerning the "New Jerusalem". In this passage, John is shown "the river of the water of life" that will flow from the throne of GOD and the LAMB. Here we see that, out of the throne of GOD, will flow a pure river of waters symbolic of HIS holiness and purity. However, this reference of a river should not be confused with the vision of Ezekiel in Ezekiel 47, or that of Zechariah in

Zechariah 14:8, as they reference a literal river flowing out of the temple at Jerusalem, in a scene set for the millennial time of CHRIST's rule here on earth. This river, in this passage, is a part of the "New Jerusalem" on the "New Earth" that GOD will ultimately create after the millennial times and the final defeat of satan. It will course its way down the center of the main street, and on each side of the river will be "a tree of life" bearing "12 crops of fruit", with a fresh crop grown each month. The leaves of those trees will be used as medicine to heal the nations of the world of all manner of sickness upon entry into the kingdom of Heaven, where there will be no more curse of illnesses of any kind.

All, who exist, will worship the FATHER, and the SON, and GOD's face will be seen by everyone for the very first time. GOD's name will also be written on their foreheads. Night will cease to exist and there will be no need for the sun, or the moon, or even lamps, because the LORD GOD will shine on everyone.

In verse 7, we find comprised, the sixth, of the seven beatitudes found in this book of Revelation, (the others are 1:3, 14:13, 16:15, 19:9, 20:6, & 22:14) which states, "Blessed are those who obey the prophecy written in this scroll". The coming of CHRIST JESUS is always "soon", in the minds of those who believe in him. A special blessing is added to those who obey and heed to the prophecy in this book of Revelation, as well as the whole of scripture itself. Indeed, we don't really love JESUS unless we are willing to obey HIM fully, take on HIS task, and take up our cross.

In Daniel 12:9, the prophet is instructed to seal up his prophesy until the time of the end. Here in revelation 22:10, the apostle John is instructed to do the opposite. He is told to "not seal up the prophetic words he has written", but rather, they are to be made available so all who wish to know and hear, can be free to do so.

In the exhortation that follows in verse 11, "let those who are doing wrong continue to do wrong, and those who do right continue to do right" is not to be taken as a "condoning of evil" by the LORD. The point of this passage does not serve to condone evil, but rather to point out the fact that, if people do not heed the prophecy in the Book of Revelation, they are only left the choice of continuing in their own wickedness. By contrast, those who do right will likely continue to do right, as GOD expects no earth-shattering changes in the conduct of mankind, good, or evil.

In, verse 12, a promise of reward and punishment is declared by the LORD, upon HIS second coming. The ALPHA and OMEGA will both reward the saints, who have benefited HIS cause, and punish those, who have hindered it. In verse 14 we see the last of the seven beatitudes of the Book of Revelation, "Blessed are those who wash their robes so they can enter in through the gates of the city and eat the fruit from the "tree of life". This is a phrase that simply describes the righteous and their acts of obedience to CHRIST's commandments. They started out guilty, but through their acceptance of CHRIST, they have been washed clean by HIS blood. On the other hand, those described in verse 11 are those who refused to give up their acts of immorality, and are thus, forever characterized by their evil ways and practices.

The SPIRIT and the Bride say come, but the lure of the World and satan say the same. The HOLY SPIRIT in us will always compel us toward CHRIST, but the "sin nature" in us will always try and tug us back toward the world. The battle within us, between the "reason to do right" and "the passion to want to do wrong" stays with us long after we accept the gift of salvation. But through our strength in CHRIST, we can overcome the gravitational pull of the world, just as CHRIST did, and find our place in the ultimate happy ending, that has been prepared for us by GOD, since the foundation of this world.

CLOSING PRAYER:

Our FATHER in Heaven, we thank YOU for being such a good GOD, a kind GOD, and, a compassionate GOD. We thank YOU for this Book of Romans, and we thank YOU for the Gospel of JESUS CHRIST. It is a wonderful, powerful message regarding the birth, life, death, burial, and resurrection of our LORD and SAVIOR. We thank YOU for YOUR great gift of salvation, through JESUS' actions and deeds, which saves us from the penalty of sin. We thank YOU for YOUR Justification, which treats us as if we never sinned at all. We thank YOU for YOUR help and guidance, by way of the HOLY SPIRIT, through our period of sanctification, and saving us from the power of sin. We thank YOU, for making it possible for us to one day enter into YOUR glorious presence, free from the presence of sin. Now LORD, we pray that this series of books will be a tool that YOU can use to bring glory and honor to YOUR Holy and righteous name. This we pray in JESUS' name. May YOUR will be done. Amen.